DIALOGUE
WITH FRIENDS

DIALOGUE WITH FRIENDS

Including
"Letters from Friends"
by Patricia Gilmore
"My Third Journey"
by Jack Powelson

HORIZON SOCIETY PUBLICATIONS
45 Bellevue Dr.
BOULDER, COLORADO 80302

Published by Horizon Society Publications, 45 Bellevue Drive, Boulder CO 80302.

PRINTED IN THE UNITED STATES OF AMERICA.

Library of Congress Cataloguing-in-Publication Data

      Powelson, John P., 1920-
      Dialogue with friends.

      Bibliography: p.
      Includes index.
      1. Church and social problems--United States. 2. Church and social problems--Society of Friends. 3. Society of Friends and world politics. 4. Society of Friends--Doctrines.
I. Title.
HN39.U6P69   1988   261.8'3   88-630
ISBN 0-9618242-1-2 (pbk.)

Table of Contents

NOTE: References are cited throughout the text in the form (Author's last name, date:page). Full information on each title is found in the section, "References cited" beginning on page 153.

Preface

After publishing *Facing Social Revolution*, I was delighted to discover that some Friends thought I had written, not a book, but a personal letter to them. As reply after reply came in, I tried to respond to each one individually. But too many piled up, so I resorted to a single letter to all.

When some said they hoped a dialogue would ensue, I invited Patricia Gilmore, an experienced journalist, to edit the letters into a one section, while I wrote about my "third journey" in another.

My first journey, through third-world countries, and my second, through history, were described in *Facing Social Revolution*.

The third journey was among Friends, during the summer of 1987 when I attended seven Quaker gatherings: Intermountain, New York, Baltimore, and New England Yearly Meetings; Friends General Conference; the Quaker Association for Economic Democracy; and Friends Association for Higher Education.

As I traveled and visited with Friends I found they wanted to discuss not only *Facing Social Revolution,* but other topics: multinational corporations; United States foreign policy; Liberation Theology; poverty in the United

States; and Nicaragua, China, and the Soviet Union. I expressed my views, and in some memorable instances Friends offered spirited challenges to them.

I had begun this journey with some trepidation, for my ideas have not been universally popular among Friends. At times I had wondered whether the Society of Friends and I had become sorely estranged. To my delight, I found that Friends came in goodly numbers to the workshops I conducted. While not all these meetings proceeded in a gentle, open-minded way, most of the time Friends were listening, talking, and loving in their consideration of how to face social revolution in non-violent ways.

I finished my third journey with joy and a renewed faith in our beloved Society of Friends. Now, in a spirit of thankfulness, I share what I have learned about Friends' present concerns; what my views are on the subjects raised; and how we may face social revolution while remaining true to our testimony for non-violence and while retaining for each other tender respect for diversities of viewpoints.

Jack Powelson

Acknowledgments

I am indebted to my sister, Louise Dudley, my wife, Robin Powelson, my son, Ken Powelson, and to Pat Gilmore, Norma Price, and Thacher Robinson for reading the manuscript and offering critical advice. Russian history professor Lawrence Silverman examined Chapter 9 on Russia and the Soviet Union, while my history student, Yan Meng, and her husband, Xiaodong Zhang, both from Beijing, did the same for Chapter 3 on China. Katherine Tokarsky did much word processing: reformatting, checking errors, and printing. Bettina Herr and Gabriela Jaramillo helped in gathering materials.

All interpretations and any errors, which I hope are few, are of course my responsibility.

LETTERS FROM FRIENDS
by Patricia Gilmore

If you have read *Facing Social Revolution,*

BEGIN HERE

If you have NOT read *Facing Social Revolution,*

we suggest you begin with "My Third Journey," Chapter 1, on page 23, and read "Letters from Friends" afterward.

Letters from Friends

He that refuseth instruction despiseth
his own soul, but he that heareth
reproof getteth understanding.

Proverbs 15:32.

So opens *Reconsiderations,* the final volume in Arnold Toynbee's *Study of History.*

"A writer and his critics are really partners in a common endeavor to increase our knowledge and understanding," says Toynbee, "and a writer ought to welcome the help that his critics are able to give him."

And so, I think, Jack Powelson shows a Toynbeean diligence in wanting his letter-writing critics to have their say in this follow-up to *Facing Social Revolution.*

The letters he received, pro and con, reveal the wisdom and wit of a wide range of Friends. As such, Jack saw them as important in themselves.

To insure a certain neutrality, he turned over to me the task of selection and asked that I add my own response.

I am indebted to the Friends quoted in this chapter, who have kindly given their permission.

- 1 -

I found sifting through Friends' letters a tender job - seeing how Jack's readers wrestled with him toward mutual enlightenment. I was tempted to arrange the material by subject. But as my interest grew in individual letters and the concerns behind them, I decided to choose a representative sample and take the letters one by one.

If there was not a meeting of minds in this correspondence, there was, I sensed, a meeting of hearts.

Quaker journalist Chuck Fager described *Facing Social Revolution* as a *cri de coeur.* As I read the response to it, I found among the writers a *cri de coeur* also.

They too were striving to hear and be heard on Friends' deepest concerns as we approach the end of the twentieth century.

Wrestling toward enlightenment

The Toynbeean analogy struck me when I read a series of letters from Scarsdale, N.Y., by Lloyd Bailey, one of the Friends who reviewed Jack's original manuscript. Lloyd tried to pin down his purpose in writing it.

> Is the purpose to attempt to clear up for yourself your profession as an economist and your profession of Quakerism, or is it an attempt to persuade . . . our Religious Society that they are guided .

. . more by emotional factors than by reason and knowledge?

Lloyd concluded that Jack would do better to devote his time to his more scholarly writings and give up a book addressed to Quakers.

His critique continued:

> When you say "many Friends feel a special warmth toward Socialist-oriented governments" . . . I believe that to be . . . a misunderstanding. [They admire certain aspects of improvement in physical conditions but do not accept a loss of political rights.] The empowerment of the poor appeals to me, [as I believe it would for most Friends.]

In response to Jack's suggestion about Friends' "loving naiveté" in economics, Lloyd countered:

> It is a charge made by every professional and every bureaucrat when change has been suggested by the non-professional . . . Friends believe . . . that Truth goes beyond statistics, reason, facts, and all of the other human endeavors made to come to sound decisions.

When I talked to Jack about Lloyd's letter, he volunteered that his early version of

Facing Social Revolution had been less sympathetic, even less tolerant, of the ideas of Friends who disagreed with him. But responses from Friends like Lloyd had helped him change his style of writing and even of thinking.

Lloyd, too, was impressed by the changes. When he read the final, printed copy of *Facing Social Revolution,* he wrote, "Jack, I really couldn't lay it down. I said to myself, is this the same book I read last fall? . . . While I found the same ideas, the presentation and tone were entirely different."

A search for serpentine wisdom, dove-like gentleness

Jack's personal journal evoked a five-page response from Alfred Andersen, a California Quaker.

> . . . Your plea, which I fully share, is that we approach our concerns with a major effort to be "wise as serpents" as well as "gentle as doves."

From his own experience as a non-governmental representative under the umbrella of the Quaker U.N. office, Al confirmed Jack's observations of third-world leaders. But he saw this leadership as part of the international scene.

> World-roving "gangs," the nation states, plunder the planet and

> its people in their acquisitiveness,
> competitiveness and combativeness .
> . . in their conspiracies in sup-
> porting each other's claims to sov-
> ereignty, even when this involves
> perpetrating horrible injustices

He said his main concern was that Jack was putting down coercion when it would be impossible to assure justice without it. "If I have to choose between injustice and coercion, I have to go with coercion."

He elaborated: "When violence takes place it usually is unjust. But not always. There are times when justice requires the use of carefully selected violence - not out of vengeance or greed, but out of compassion."

> Our challenge is to develop
> the Inward Light, both individually
> and as a group, to where we intui-
> tively *feel* what coercion *is* morally
> justified or required. . .

Though he himself was so disenchanted with the U.S. government he hadn't filed a tax return for four decades, he believed Jack's rejection of all coercion reflected a basic inconsistency in the position of many Friends.

As for economic solutions for an ideal society, he liked Jack's idea of receiving a share in the profit from the nation's collective capital, besides the income from one's own work. But he believed the basic way to achieve what he called "fair share capitalism" was to share in

the income from a "fair rent for the use of the
land and its resources, our common heritage"
which no one would then own (Andersen 1985).

Like many other readers, Al criticized
Jack's statement that "social change occurs by
gradual increments in the strength of the poor
themselves. . . "

> Again, this seems to me laying
> too much on the oppressed and let-
> ting the rest of us remain too aloof
> in our privileged ivory towers . . .
> To relate this matter (of who takes
> the initiative) to the issue of co-
> ercion in the face of extreme social
> oppression seems the ultimate in the
> worst kind of paternalism.

The Third-World Experienced

A number of letters came from Friends with
first-hand experience in the third world.

One of these, Louise Wilson, a retired
social worker from Palo Alto, had traveled to
Cuba and Jamaica with Oxfam America to study
contrasting ways of food production. She found
that Jack's experience reinforced her own con-
clusions on non-violence, on supporting the
needy in taking charge of their own lives, and
on the futility of giving from the top down.
But:

> I wished you had recognized
> that we have been responsible for a
> good many ills through our lending

policies, emphasis on export crops vs. home consumption, clearing rain forest, political manipulation by the CIA, etc. . .

My observation is that in Nicaragua and Cuba, for example, the poor have been able to make permanent involvement in their economic welfare in spite of political repression and that these governments have often favored and protected these advances . . . I believe the base communities in Nicaragua which have been flourishing since before the revolution are a tremendous force for learning and energizing . . .

I believe the Nicaraguan government has realized its mistakes with the East Coast Indians and that by use of conflict resolution processes the problems of autonomy were being worked out.

Andy Towl, of Cambridge (Massachusetts) Meeting, received *Facing Social Revolution* just as he was being solicited for development work in India. Reading it reminded him of his experiences in other countries, including Kenya where he first met Jack.

He sympathized with Jack's frustration in believing he had done more harm than good in his third-world advising, but he went on:

Even in Kenya, each of us may have done more good than we realize. The leverage of the poor, which you argue for and with good reason, may be more effective if the government has a better perspective from you and your counterparts . . . It is a slow process.

Andy joined in Jack's concern that we risk abandoning our principles when we ally ourselves with groups according to their ends, rather than the means to achieve them.

On resolving conflict, he queried: "Is not the basis for creative negotiation the clarification of interests in common?"

A Friend from Albuquerque identified with the first chapter of *Facing Social Revolution* (dealing with bureaucratic frustration in Kenya), which "reminded me of my own experience in different countries in Africa."

Rebecca Cresson of Monte Verde, Costa Rica, shared Jack's belief in the capacities of the poor. She told of her son's experience with the "less privileged - or perhaps less fettered" in researching literacy techniques:

His assistant is a young man who only completed 6th grade [but is] observant, innovative and very adept, quite able to understand and use complicated information.

I am a great supporter of formal education but realize that we are apt to miss the potentials and usefulness of other types of learning. Is [formal education] another facet of the power or ascendancy drive?

From the Philippines came a letter from Tony de Jesus, who said he and his wife chose to be in "development" via the health field:

We started our involvement with much emotion and we were willing to embrace any and all means to "champion" the cause of the oppressed. We have re-evaluated our contribution over the past years. We have learned to look at historical evolution . . .

A Vermont Friend who had worked with the Methodist Church in Mexico and Peru was less sympathetic with *Facing Social Revolution*. She and other Friends who had been studying the book believed that Jack was not "in touch with reality."

Involved in both the peace and sanctuary movements, she has been troubled by the tension between the Quaker peace testimony and the revolutions for social justice. On behalf of her study group, she wrote:

The poor have not been granted their just share of the wealth. Their only power of leverage (which you recommend) is joining in legal and illegal protest for change. We support revolution when other means have been tried to no avail. We point to the U.S. revolution, Russian, French, Cuban and now Central American as successful (knowing the imperfections). We also support sanctions in South Africa . . .

As a Quaker I wonder why you do not support liberation theology which essentially recognized the "inner light" of each person and the need to lift all from oppression.

As much as she disagreed with Jack, she too sought common ground:

We appreciate your study, agree with the dilemma of the peace testimony and violent revolutions, agree with your principles, and strongly disagree with your devaluation of boycotts, sanctions, liberation theology . . . It appears we will continue to live with this tension.

Gratitude for expressing an unpopular view

Donald Bybee, clerk of an eastern Meeting, found solace in Jack's courage in speaking out:

I think you are positively correct in your views regarding the rationale and focus of Quaker activ-

ism. Your views here are so much
like my own which before your book
I'd thought were unique to me among
Friends. . . fated to be seen as
recklessly at variance with the lib-
eral dogma which is so second nature
to so many Friends.

Challenging Jack's view of history

In a lively intellectual parrying with
Jack, Hugh Chapman, a Friend from Pennsylvania,
wrote:

There is one problem for me
with your thesis. Time used to take
care of things better than now. . .

The threat of atomic attacks
by fanatics or terrorists or irre-
sponsible governments worries me;
and the atomic threat is so dreadful
and can produce such disastrous consequences that I wonder if we can
wait for people with good sense to
become empowered . . .

Another letter with a contrasting look
came from a Tennessee Friend, Larry Ingle. He
was not sure he agreed with Jack's economic pre-
scriptions: "As a non-economist I am unable to
evaluate [them] on the same terms as you do."
But as a writer on Quaker history he argued that
Jack's reading of the rise of Quakerism was off
the mark:

While early Friends may not
have had explicit programs to deal
for example with poverty - even
this, however, we cannot be sure of,
for the work in this area still re-
mains to be done - the fact that
Levellers and Diggers like Winstan-
ley became Friends after the collapse of their secular schemes sug-
gests that they saw Quakerism as a
way to preserve their early efforts
. . .

Of course they did not tackle
complex matters; they endeavored to
live lives of faithfulness, which
inevitably led them to confront the
political powers that be. So if you
want an image of apolitical people,
you need to look to others - perhaps
the Presbyterians when they were
close to power.

Enough. I found your book pro-
vocative and its point of view chal-
lenging.

Readable text or complex rhetoric?

Most Friends who commented on the language
of *Facing Social Revolution* thanked Jack for his
simplicity of style. They liked the way he put
technical information and complex ideas into
readable terms.

Judy Inskeep, from New York Yearly Meeting, brought a background in the Peace Corps and a desire to understand Jack's economic analysis:

> I am halfway through your book, and am finding it not only challenging but readable. (I was afraid it might not be, based on my fear of economics!)

But California Friend Lee McKusick, bothered by ambiguities, didn't agree.

> *Facing Social Revolution* has complex rhetoric. It is extremely difficult to write you a letter. I receive your message warmly and I feel some emergency over the good intention and complexity of the rhetoric.

A scathing rebuttal

Clifford Proctor, an articulate Quaker in Vermont, responded to *Facing Social Revolution* with a scathing rebuttal. He was a member of the group mentioned above that thought Jack was "out of touch with reality." He wrote:

> Attendance was five at the first weekly meeting (although others had also purchased copies . .), and three at the second meeting. The project was abandoned. . .
>
> In my youth, there was a popular song entitled, "I Can't Get

Started with You." We couldn't get
started with you.

. . . Your facts and insights,
we thought, were stated sensational-
ly - that is, in a manner designed
to evoke dissent. . . "He can't really mean that" or "That can't be
true". . .

Are we really able to measure
Zambia's food production to the
nearest one-hundredth of one percent? Indeed, can we make an annual
estimate of the population of Zambia
that accurately, to compute per capita figures? . . .

Finally, (re Chapter 10, "The
Myth of the Ignorant Poor"), . . .
we seem to have here an economist's
equivalent of the philosopher's noble savage. Does the Guatemalan peasant really know that the University of Iowa has hybridized his crop
to make it resist blight and yield
50% more for the same labor? Does he
know whether a marketing cooperative
would help? Or whether a dam to ir-
rigate his entire valley is feasible, and what it would do to communities downstream?

Reviewers note shared values, varied conclusions

Friends' reviews of Friends' publications
often throw extra light on Friends' issues. They

usually reflect a thoughtful cross-section of Quakerdom, making a conscientious effort to understand a writing and offer a response.

Carol Reilley Urner, who reviewed *Facing Social Revolution* for *Quaker Life*, wrote Jack a personal letter as well. "At the root I think we see much the same when it comes to basic values," she said. But she also wrote:

> I still come away with a sense that you feel we, who are rich, can just sort of go ahead with our own comfortable lives and let the poor and history take care of social change. But I know you don't really feel that way . . .

> I think the social and economic programs the world has seen have been purchased with love, blood and tears by those who have given all they have and are in the continuing nonviolent struggle for truth and justice. . . Everything we have and are is also required to lift oppression and heal the wounds of oppressor and oppressed alike.

This appeared to be a common thread among the critics: on the one side the oppressed, on the other the oppressors. If you are not the oppressed, you are probably among the oppressors.

Carol called Jack into question for not fully recognizing "the radical nature of the

revolution into which we ourselves are called."
She proposed an antidote: Woolman's *Plea for
the Poor* and the Gospel of Luke as it suggested
to her the views of Jesus on economics and social justice.

For *Quaker Life,* she pinpointed one part
of the problem for Friends:

> Jack has long been concerned
> by what he perceives as a drift away
> from our Quaker values among some
> more "liberal" Friends. He senses
> that there is at times a willingness
> to condone violence on behalf of the
> poor, and a readiness to support
> those centralist third world govern-
> ments that impose socialist solu-
> tions from above. He is sure - and
> somehow I think most Friends would
> share his certainties - that we
> Friends cannot abandon the way of
> non-violence.

She was not comfortable with Jack's historical analysis, for she thought he ignored
Toynbee's "gentle proletariat." But she shared
his view of the importance of individual, every-
day actions over time.

> In those centuries (11th-13th)
> thousands of men and women - Catho-
> lic Franciscans and Humiliati as
> well as "heretic" Waldensians and
> Cathars - rediscovered the gospels
> and the Spirit of Christ within.
> Like early Friends they abjured

oath-taking and bearing arms, and thus cut at the foundations of the feudal system.

Tom Head, in a review of *Facing Social Revolution* in *Evangelical Friend,* wrote:

> [Jack's] concerns about the biases of Quakers are most frequently appropriate to that (unprogrammed) branch of the Quaker movement. Evangelical Friends often have another set of biases about which to be reflective. So, in some of his specific conclusions he may not speak to the condition of all Friends, but I believe that his general example and admonition to examine our biases speaks to us all. If, in attempting to translate our faith into action, we can all be as reflective about our personal journey as Jack Powelson has been about his, we will do well.

Allen Stokes, a Utah Friend, reviewed *Facing Social Revolution* for *Logan Friends Newsletter.* After describing Jack's ideas about how to achieve economic justice, he wrote:

> In the course of his book Jack challenges and refutes many of our cherished dogma and widely-held stereotypes about the wealthy . . . the poor and the sharing of wealth. You may try to squirm out of your comfortable positions, but to me Jack's

reasoned, objective development of
his position makes good reading for
Friends.

Then there was Chuck Fager's review for *A
Friendly Letter*. He described Jack's ideas about
how to get economic justice - the slow, moderat-
ing growth of institutions that incorporate conflict resolution, compromise, and decentraliza-
tion of power. He concluded:

> During the Vietnam years, such
> talk seemed utterly inadequate and
> irrelevant to me and many of my
> peers. Today most of it makes a
> great deal of sense . . . Does that
> mean I am now wiser or merely older?

Twentieth century lessons

As the lessons of the twentieth century
sink in, Friends may well become wiser with age,
not just individually but as a Religious Society
seeking truth for almost 350 years. This thought
struck me as I reread my own review of *Facing
Social Revolution* for *Friends' Bulletin*. In it,
I quoted peace researcher Kenneth Boulding, from
a Boulder Friends discussion of the book:

> What Jack is worrying about is
> how to do good. Good will is not
> enough. Good skill is what is need-
> ed. How do we mobilize good skills
> in the Society of Friends, in a
> world that is a complex, total sys-
> tem?

Kenneth spoke of our striving to mend the world, to heal its wounds. Healing, he suggested, means that when something goes wrong there is a thermostat giving accurate *feedback* to make it go right.

Otherwise, he said, we may get the feeling we're doing good when actually we're doing harm. Ideologies can lead to that feeling.

I think this feedback problem is why Jack asks us to take a closer look at "just wars" and liberation movements, whether at home or abroad. A worthy cause can defeat its goal by the process it uses to get there.

As a movement gathers steam and passion, as it develops a creed and party line, ends can come to justify means. Angry confrontations and violence may replace the search for common ground.

Questioning is questioned. Adverse fallout is ignored.

The Problem of the P.G.Q.

A more serious problem for Friends, it seems to me, is the tendency to level value judgments against the non-converted. A sort of Political Goodness Quotient emerges.

This P.G.Q. tends to type and evaluate Friends, and others, according to the "rightness" of their political advocacy. It looks at people according to their social action prefer-

ences rather than their personal humanity or
ethical practices.

At a deeper level, agreement

My conclusion in looking back over this
material is that at a deeper level Friends agree
more than they differ. Friends all want to relieve suffering. They simply differ on how.

That's not to say differences aren't important. Take the matter of the pie, for example. Many Friends see the world's goods as a
static pie. What one person has another has to
do without. We all share one home, planet earth,
and should seek to distribute its goods equally.

Jack, on the other hand, sees an expanda-
ble pie. It grows with development - not just
tools and management skills, but certain habits-
of-the-heart that become imbedded in the culture. Friends knew and traditionally practiced
these habits in both more and less developed
countries, with economic success as a surprising
byproduct.

What Jack and various Friends propose to
do about poverty springs from their respective
views of that pie. In setting out to dialogue
with Friends by way of journal and journey, Jack
has sought a Quaker way to deal with these different understandings.

What makes us better?

One of the letters Jack received came from
Irwin Abrams, coordinator of the newly estab-

lished Quaker Studies in Human Betterment. This organization gathers scholars together for a rigorous examination of how things go from good to better or from bad to worse. Irwin considered Jack's search to be along this line and welcomed his input.

Kenneth Boulding, one of the founders of QSHB, said in the Afterword to *Facing Social Revolution:*

> The distinction between right and left has blurred. The time is ripe for new inquiries into what makes for human betterment.

Through the process of criticism and reconsideration, Jack and his critics become part of that inquiry into human betterment.

MY THIRD JOURNEY
by Jack Powelson

Chapter One

Perceptions of Change:
Forty-Five Years
in the Society of Friends

How should I respond to the many fervent and fertile ideas expressed in Pat Gilmore's section, "Letters from Friends?" Virtually all the ideas in these letters came up again during my third journey, so I will take them up in the story of that journey, which begins in Chapter 2.

One idea persistently came to my mind as the journey progressed. How the Society of Friends has changed in the forty-five years of my membership! While I did not dwell on these changes in my workshops, they lay at the kernel of my thinking, so it is appropriate to start "My third journey" with them.

First Change: Tolerance of Political Diversity

When I joined the Society of Friends in 1943, the political composition of my Meeting (New York) was more balanced than is that of my Meeting (Boulder) today. Solid Republicans sat in the New York benches. Friends would vote for Dewey as readily as for Roosevelt. Some grumbled

- 23 -

about how "that man" (Roosevelt) had packed the
Supreme Court and about the fiscal irresponsibi-
lity of the New Deal.

Our sensitivity to injustice was personal
rather than institutional.

We recalled the beginnings of the American Friends Service Committee, not as an organization but as people who fed German children
after World War I. Later Friends had helped ref-
ugees of the Spanish civil war and had fed hungry people in France. Some Friends were intern-
ed at Baden Baden during World War II when the
Germans overran France.

At home during the late 1940s, Friends
protested against racial injustice, sitting in
restaurants alongside black friends, refusing to
leave until served. Week-end work camps offered
ways for individual Friends to improve deprived
neighborhoods in Philadelphia.

The AFSC mobilized young Friends to help
reconstruct European villages after the war and
to combat poverty in Mexico.

Besides pacifism and race relations, which
I will address later in this chapter, the main
political issues were whether to join the United
Nations and how it would be structured; world
federalism; the Marshall Plan; foreign aid; labor relations, including the minimum wage and
support for unions; and farm programs and
prices.

But a Friend who would keep us out of the United Nations because the League had failed was just as valued as one who saw the U.N. as a positive step toward world government. A Friend who opposed the minimum wage because it might cause unemployment was considered just as moral as one who favored it.

No Friend was deemed less sensitive to the poor because of a particular political position taken.

Friends have been divided politically many times in the past, such as during the American Revolution, the abolitionist and Civil War period, and in World War I. Political differences may have underlain some of our historic splits.

I joined the Friends at a time of healing, however, when Hicksite and Orthodox Yearly Meetings were recombining. I have always thought of Friends as able to embrace widely divergent political persuasions.

But ten years ago, a young couple left Boulder Meeting because they were uncomfortable among pro-abortionists. Forthcoming rallies for the Democratic candidate and protests against nuclear power have been announced at the rise of the Meeting.

When Judge Bork was nominated for the Supreme Court, a petition opposing him was circulated after Meeting.

The AFSC has issued many documents favoring political positions in the third world that

I have questioned in *Facing Social Revolution* and question again in *Dialogue with Friends.*

Many Friends speak of the policies of socialist governments as if they were unquestionably right, implying that those like myself, who disagree, are uninformed or insensitive.

During my third journey I encountered other Friends who were troubled by our seeming politicization. At New York Yearly Meeting, Joshua Brown circulated a document, "You Can't Get There from Here, . . ." which spoke of the narrowing base of Friends, economically, culturally, and politically. In it he asked, "Is God a Democrat? If not, can a Friend be a Republican?"

If we respect the Inner Lights of those who disagree with us politically, can we not harbor a Friend who, believing that life is sacred, opposes abortion? Or a Friend who sees nuclear power as a means of rescuing peoples of the third world from their poverty?

Or one who favored Judge Bork as legally qualified to serve on the Supreme Court? Or one who believes that the government of Nicaragua is harming the poor with its pricing policies more than it helps them?

People of those beliefs are found in other churches. What has happened to them among Friends? Have we driven them away? Or - as I would guess - has the fertility of our soil so changed that they do not take root when they visit us or hear of us? Does their absence make our Society more vigorous, or more narrow?*

Second Change: Friends Divided on Pacifism

New York Young Friends were divided on pacifism in 1943. Some went to war, others drove ambulances on the battlefield. Some were drafted into civilian public service camps; others went to prison. Some offered themselves for medical experiments; some worked in mental hospitals.

The Young Friends whom I joined were conscientious objectors, because those who were not were overseas. How did we feel about those who went to war? To refresh my memory, I looked up an editorial I wrote in the *Young Friends Correspondent,* September 1943:

> But these men whom we call militarists have ideals of their own. . . they feel they are fighting for freedom . . They are guilty of the inability to understand the viewpoint of conscientious ˀbjectors, many of whom they feel to be slackers . . . But are we not guilty

----

*I speak for my own branch of Friends. The same political changes may not have occurred in other branches. Nor do my examples necessarily apply to Meetings other than my own.

Furthermore, nothing in this section should be taken as questioning the value of the Friends Committee on National Legislation. I support the FCNL strongly. The FCNL has listened carefully to all political opinions expressed by Friends and has lobbied only on issues on which its supporting Meetings have been in unity.

> of not understanding them? . . We
> are not fighting *against* these men;
> we are fighting *for* them and *for* the
> ideals they are fighting for.

Not every conscientious objector agreed
with this editorial. But we were agreed that the
Allied cause was just and the Germans were
wrong: no one condoned armies overrunning Europe
or the gassing of Jews.

The question was only whether war against
these atrocities was moral. A secondary question
was whether it would be effective.

Perhaps the change came with the Vietnam
war. Most of us opposed it, yet I believe its
effect was to make us more militant than pacifist.

Friends who speak today of "peace and justice" seem to me more akin to those who went to
war in the 1940s than to those who were pacifist. Why?

Possibly because now our country seems to
many Friends to be on the side of injustice - as
in Vietnam or Nicaragua - not justice as in
World War II.

The division of Friends today, on whether
we would fight in a social revolution, has a
contrasting quality from that of the 1940s. In
the 1940s, every pacifist I knew would have resisted *nonviolently* had the Germans invaded our
country. Increasingly today, Friends equivocate
on whether social oppression in the third world

can be overcome nonviolently. Often they say "justice first, then peace."

As we put up our blackout curtains during World War II and read about saturation bombing in Europe, we were well aware of what the Germans and Japanese might do to us. We reassured each other on the exercise of nonviolence in the face of military attack.

But today, even though the Soviet Union once placed nuclear weapons in Cuba, many Friends speak as if it would never do so in Nicaragua.

Does our pacifism now rely on presuming that the foe is gentle rather than on standing peaceful before violence?

Are Friends joining mainline Christianity, which historically has advocated the "just war?"

Third Change: Color Blind or Color Conscious

While a graduate student in the late 1940s, I was resource person, lecturer, and square dance caller at AFSC summer institutes of international affairs. We tried hard, with some success, to attract Blacks to these institutes. Our discussions on race relations centered not on laws but on personal attitudes.

Our goal was to be "color blind." We would tell the story of Joey, a white boy in a border neighborhood, who spoke often of his good friend Jimmy. Knowing that Blacks were in his school, Joey's parents asked him one day, "Is Jimmy black?" Joey replied, "I don't know. Next time I see him, I'll look." I tell this story not because I think you haven't heard it, but because it typified the era.

Two major differences mark the late 1980s. One is that the quest for racial equality became political, a matter for Congress and the courts. The other is that ethnic minorities assumed their identities. "Color blind" was out. "Black is beautiful" was in.

I favor both these changes, yet I am uneasy. I no longer want to be color blind, but I do not want to be color conscious either. Having worked for international agencies and lived many years abroad, I accept people of other countries as human beings, recognizing their differences as they recognize that I am different from them.

I want to learn their languages so I can speak with them. I want to know their cultures so I will not be a stranger in their homes. I do not want to give up my identity, and I do not expect them to give up theirs.

But I do not want to magnify our differences.

I feel similarly about ethnic minorities in my own country. I am uneasy when persons of an ethnic minority resent my not having "noticed" their ethnicity, as happened once on my third journey.

I fear that forging ethnic blocs to promote identity may instead cause confrontations.

I do not agree with the AFSC's establishing ethnic quotas on its staff, because I feel they make too much of differences. I want to assume a more natural relationship among equals.

Many Friends are disturbed that racial injustice has not ended. They are disappointed that changing the law does not immediately change hearts and minds. But the hearts and minds of *many* people have changed.

Yet I still hear some Friends and persons of ethnic minorities acting as if nothing has been accomplished, and expressions of guilt are numerous.

Fourth Change: Does Greed Lie in Business or in People?

When I joined the Friends, I was fresh out of the Wharton School of Finance and Commerce with an MBA. I had won a prize for my thesis, in which I invented a cost-accounting system for railway freight. My ambition was to be personnel officer for a railroad.

In the meantime, I was a junior accountant, taking orders from my seniors and checking vouchers against embezzlement.

I considered my career honorable and instructive. Business met human needs and provided jobs.

An accountant would read the story of a business in its records the way other people would read a story in a book. Either could be exciting.

Other Friends were in business too, and I recall that our careers were esteemed. Only when my old professor at Wharton called me back to teach accounting did I consider going into education.

Earlier Friends were also businesspeople, in manufacturing, banking, transportation, and services. They were concerned that their products should be of high quality and truthfully represented.

Quakers established the practice of fixed prices, because it was not honest to quote one price and sell at another, or to sell to one person at one price and to another at another. Children might be sent to a Quaker shop, for no haggling was required and the shopkeeper would not cheat them.

On December 31, 1943, my boss, a partner in the firm, pulled me off my current audit and assigned me to the year-end inventory count of Winchester Repeating Arms. But I could not do what he asked, for Winchester was supplying war materiel. That afternoon I went to his office and submitted my resignation.

It was not accepted, for accountants were scarce in wartime. Instead, I was relieved of the inventory count, and I called square dances at the Young Friends' New Year's Eve party. Two days later, I felt embarrassed that my fellow workers had toiled on New Year's eve while I

frolicked. But I felt I had done right in af-
firming the Quaker peace testimony.

I am not sure when anti-business sentiment
invaded the Society of Friends. When I first
sensed it, I was dismayed, for it seemed to de-
personalize me.

It was not *business* that made early Quakers sell at a fixed price; it was *they* who de-
fined the terms of business. Whether I audited
Winchester was *my* decision. No one could make me
do it or not do it.

Anti-business sentiment is neither new nor
peculiar to Friends.

Many innovations that have
passed economic tests successfully
have been met by efforts to make
them unlawful: the joint-stock company; the department store; the
mail-order house; the chain store;
the trusts; the integrated process
enterprise; the branch bank; the
conglomerate; the multinational corporation (Rosenberg and Birdzell
1986:309).

I suspect that three forces underlie the
anti-business sentiment growing in our Society
since 1943.

One is our increased involvement, as a
nation, in the third world and our perception
that multinational corporations perpetrate injustices there.

Another is a perception of socialism and cooperatives as humanistic alternatives to profit-seeking business.

Still another possibility is that there may *be* fewer businesspeople in the Society of Friends and more academics. Has anyone counted?

I believe anti-business sentiment is part of a larger tendency among Friends to judge a "system" - whether business or government - as moral or immoral, and to view persons operating within that system as mere pawns absolved of moral accountability.

I emphasize "tendency," for this is no polar construct. If socialism is good, we think that those who operate within it *tend* to be good. If multinational corporations are bad, those who manage them *tend* to be bad.

At the same time that we attribute greed to "the system," I believe we tend to treat capitalism as "more greedy" than it really is and socialism as "less greedy" than it really is. I will explain this statement by examples later in the book.

If we are accountable for our moral conduct no matter what the operating framework, then the "system" ceases to be moral or immoral, and responsibility is returned to the person. With this viewpoint, we are freed to think of business, socialism, capitalism, and government for what they are: reflections of the qualities of the people who guide and operate them.

I do not deny the culture of systems, or the judgment that some systems are better than others. A soldier's moral choices are limited by the culture of the army. An employee of a business must not contravene that business's welfare. We all feel intense pressures to conform.

But it is not that we either are or are not subject to the system. It is that some of us allow ourselves to be more subject than others. Some are more willing than others to take the penalty for civil disobedience.

The private does not *have* to obey the sergeant even if death is the penalty for not doing so. Nor does the employee *have* to do what the boss says even if being sacked is the result.

The acceptance of personal moral responsibility *even in an adverse system* has been a historic hallmark of Friends. George Fox, James Naylor, William Penn, John Lilburne, and John Woolman all acted according to their own consciences and not according to the systems in which they were thrown.

So did the thousands who defied the Inquisition. So did the Jews of the Middle Ages who chose torture rather than forced conversion to Christianity. When Jesus said, "Render unto Caesar, . . ." I believe he was speaking to this point.

There is no virtue in being good if the system requires it of us. Nor is there any fault in being evil if the system forces us. Thus we cannot conceive of individual morality unless we cease to abdicate responsibility for our actions to some "system," whatever its form may be. By the same token, we will never change a system unless the people within it change first.

Fifth Change: Perceptions of National Power

In 1942, Germany occupied much of western Europe and was cutting slices out of the Soviet Union. Japan was entrenched in most of urban China and in vast areas of southeast Asia. Many Americans thought we would lose the war.

We remembered how difficult it had been to overcome a decade-long depression. We wondered whether America's peak of power had passed.

Once the war had been won, however, the belief in a powerful United States was revived. The Soviet Union would be contained by the Truman doctrine. We would prevent the spread of communism in Vietnam, and we would control events in Latin America. Third-world countries would fall in with whatever policies our government should see fit.

Strangely, this view of a powerful United States is shared by political opposites: the American government and the Society of Friends. The main difference is that our government believes its actions are moral while many Friends find them immoral.

Neither group, it seems to me, has come to grips with the reality that our world power has been significantly diminished while that of Ja-

pan and third-world governments has been enor-
mously increased.

The international weakness of the United
States is reflected in our trade deficit and our
fiscal deficit. We are now a net debtor nation.

We could not win a war in Vietnam. We
cannot control events in Central America. We are
powerless when Iranians attack ships in the Per-
sian Gulf. We no longer influence Cuba, though
it sits but ninety miles from us.

Our multinational corporations and banks
have been nationalized by third-world governments, one after another. We no longer own oil
companies in the Middle East, Indonesia, or Venezuela. All our banks in Mexico are lost.

We cannot persuade the Argentines, the
Brazilians, the Mexicans, or the Peruvians to
follow economic policies we consider salutary.

In January, 1988, Spain forced us to re-
move 72 jet fighters from our air base there. We
tremble at revolution in the Philippines, which
might deprive us of key bases overseeing the
Pacific, for which, in the opinion of our military, there are no substitutes.

None of this would have been considered
remotely possible in 1945.

The same distortion applies to our perception of the third world. In country after country in Asia and Africa, a small élite has re-
placed the colonial powers.

These élites have overtaxed their poor. They have sucked the agricultural surplus from small farmers and driven them to the edge of starvation, weakening food output so the rest of the people are also hungry.

They have destroyed their ecologies far more than we have our own. They have engaged in civil wars to quash their political foes and international wars to augment their borders.

Yet I sense a tendency among Friends to believe that these governments are benign but weak before the overwhelming power of the United States.

The main purpose of *Facing Social Revolution* was, in some sense, to awaken the Society of Friends to the new reality.

A few Friends in my third journey understood. One who had served in Burkina Faso said to me, "When I read *Facing Social Revolution,* I knew on every page what you were talking about, because I had been there."

But other Friends looked on me as obsessed with my perception of today's reality, a person to be humored but not taken seriously.

Still others - most, I like to believe - took pause and said they would think it over. For this, I express my humble thanks and offer this continuing dialogue so that Friends may search for the Truth together.

Chapter Two

My Heavy Burden

"You bear a heavy burden. You defend the rich and the powerful, whose greed causes wars and suffering for faceless millions. You have maligned good people who stand on the front lines to help the poor and defenseless. Your values are twisted. When your time comes you will have much to answer for."

In a vibrant, quaking voice, suggestive of a Quaker elder of yesteryear, a Friend solemnly admonished me in these approximate words. About 60 Friends were gathered in a circle, and I stood in the center. We were at one of two workshops on *Facing Social Revolution* at Friends General Conference in Oberlin Ohio.

It was an awesome experience. Not knowing when or how to respond, I called for a moment of silence. Moments later, another Friend spoke, saying she felt much the same as the preceding speaker but would not have expressed it so strongly.

I sensed that about a third of those present agreed with the vibrant Friend and were militant in their feelings. Another third agreed but in softened tones, while a third group seemed more sympathetic to my messages. Approximately the same proportions held for the other workshop, also with 60 Friends in attendance.

Until this occasion, I had thought I didn't care how Friends felt about me personally. I would speak what I thought was right and true, and if Friends found me callous, that was the price I had to pay for my convictions. But in the silence after our Friend's pronouncement, I recognized I had been hurt.

On impulse, I asked, "How many of you think I care for the poor?" More than half the hands went up. While I was relieved at their response, I was concerned that so many Friends had not raised their hands.

After the meeting was over, I took a long, solitary walk. Why, I asked myself, did this Friend find me so callous, so uncaring? Why was I hurt by his judgment?

I thought of the times I had walked through the slums and over small farms in Latin America, Asia, and Africa; of the times I had talked to poor people and to radical students who were concerned for them. But in these reminiscences I was only indulging myself, trying to prove to myself that that Friend was wrong.

No, I realized, I needed to know why these Friends and I perceived my concern so differently and what if anything I could do to build bridges to my militant critics.

I thought of what other Friends, close friends who wanted to help me, had said on other occasions. "Jack, you're too intellectual. You have been too long a teacher. Friends work from feelings. You don't persuade them with arguments or facts."

I had tossed out this idea, for I had always believed that most Friends were found among intellectuals. This might even have been one of our weaknesses, I had thought. Now my thinking went into reverse.

In the silence of that walk, I struggled with the dilemma: when is one to be led by one's emotional response, and when is one called upon to use the reasoning facilities with which God has endowed us?

Obviously, God does not tell us facts. God does not analyze situations for us. But God does give us a spirit with which to be sensitive to certain types of "knowing" and a mind with which to analyze facts and to arrive at reasoned judgments and plans of action. We can "know" certain types of things by being led by the Inner Light, and we can "know" other types by using our minds for critical analysis and assessment.

But how do we distinguish between those two types?

Possibly our first feelings, our emotions, may lead us into hasty, inappropriate responses.

Our inner voice that cries out with anguish for the poor may mislead us.

It is not enough to talk to the poor and to live with them. We must also use our faculties for analyzing the causes and possible routes out of poverty.

My reasoning self says one must understand the policies of governments. One must know the full impact of an economic action and not just its immediate results. One must have some historical understanding of what has led to this time and condition.

In that solitary walk, I knew I might fault myself, as others had, for sounding too cold and intellectual. But intellectual I had to be, or I would fail to use the faculty for analytical thinking that God had given me.

Others might arrive at ways of "knowing" acceptable to them. I would accept their sincerity and would hope in time to win theirs for mine. But if not, so be it. With that, I found some sense of consolation.

That afternoon had been a quaking experience, but later in the week I received some comforting words. As I walked across the Oberlin campus, at least five Friends stopped me on separate occasions to comment on Friends' reactions.

"They were not listening to you," these Friends told me. "They cut you off before you had finished sentences. They thought they knew what you were going to say before you said it."

One Friend pinned a note for me on the message board:

> I am saddened that the passions of our militant zealots of non-violence obscured your message until the evening's hour was late.

One of the "militant zealots" also stopped me on the campus. "I had not read *Facing Social Revolution* when I made my remarks," he said. "Now I have. Had I done so earlier, I would have spoken differently."

If I have much to answer for when my time comes, let it be because after investigating as best I could, after being scientific as well as human, still I have erred. Let it not be *either* because I failed to investigate thoroughly or scientifically *or* because I did not listen to that voice calling for humility and humanity.

Chapter Three

China

Did not China, some Friends asked, belie my assertion in *Facing Social Revolution* that violent revolution always recreates the previous society? China, they said, had conquered famine and had brought education and improved the lives of the poor.

I can only consider that question in the context of the last three millennia.

China's present revolution has been enacted many times, and always the earlier society has been re-created. Over and again for 3,000 years new Chinese governments have instituted waves of reforms in the name of peasants.

Lands have been repeatedly confiscated from the lords and divided among the poor.

The Zhou dynasty of 1050 BC divided the land into plots of nine fields in a three-by-three matrix. Each of eight farmers along the four sides was given a field for family use. They cultivated the ninth (center) field in common, paying the produce to the state to feed the army and the administrators.

Although the Han (206 BC) had confiscated all lands and given them to the nobility, the Emperor Wang Mang, usurper of that dynasty, took them back in 9 AD and divided them among the peasants.

The Northern Wei established the "equal-field-allocation system," which the Sui and Tang copied when they unified China in the seventh century. All the land of China was divided equally among those of working age, who would return the fields for re-allocation when they were too old to farm.

Canals were built and crops transported and stored in "ever-normal" granaries around the country, so no one would starve.

Relative to contemporary technology, the Tang of a millennium and a half ago had done as much to feed and advance their poor as the revolutionary government has done today.

Centuries after the Tang, the Sung emperor offered credit and supplies to small farmers and fed them during famines. More centuries later, the Ming emperor confiscated land from the gentry and divided it among the peasants.

But why did the Tang dynasty have to do again what the Zhang, the Wei, and the Sui dynasties had done? Why did the Sung have to do what the Tang had done? The Ming what the Sung had done? And the People's Republic what the Ming dynasty had done?

Why did the reforms not last?

All these reforms had four elements in common. First, the reforming government had come into power by war. Second, the peasants received land only if they gave its product, above what they needed for subsistence, to the government, to support its armies and its bureaucrats. Third, the government set the prices of food-stuffs and fertilizer in its own favor. Fourth, the emperor's power invited envy.

Threatened by court intrigues, rebellious warlords, or invasions from the north, to protect themselves the emperors retook the land from small farmers. They gave it to favorites who would defend them. Wars from within or invasions from outside brought down each dynasty and started the cycle afresh.

Over and again, across the centuries, the scenario was played, each time with its own variations, but each time essentially the same. Chinese historians were first to identify the dynastic cycle, describing it much as I just did.

Is the People's Republic something new in history? Or does it mark the beginning of a new dynastic cycle?

Let us examine the elements.

First, the government took power by war.

Second, without approval from the peasantry it organized cooperatives, then collective farms, then communes, which have been required to sell their output to the government at prices set by it.

Third, the government owns monopolies of all major production: mining, steel, and foreign trade.

Fourth, a great power struggle ensued in the Cultural Revolution of the 1960s. It is not yet over. Since then, the Mao cult has been displaced. The "gang of four" is in prison. Both the originator of the Revolution and his wife have been disgraced.

All the elements of the historic cycles are present today.

Furthermore, the land confiscated by the People's Republic was *not* the large estates of powerful owners, as was the case in Latin America.

In the centuries after the Ming reform, farm plots became fragmented by equal inheritance. By the twentieth century China was a country of small farms.

When Pearl Buck's husband (1937:197) studied 16,786 farms in 22 provinces, he found an average size of 5.36 acres in the wheat region and 3.09 acres in the rice region, without much variation. Other writers (e.g., Harvard Sinologist Perkins 1969) confirm the small sizes.

Buck also found that "somewhat less than three-fourths of the land is owned by the farmer himself and one-fourth is rented" (p.194). He therefore concluded, before the revolution of 1949, that "the extent of farm tenancy in China is no greater than in many other countries" (p.196).

Furthermore, most of the tenancy was in the south. Indeed, most northern areas had no tenants at all. Why the difference, Perkins (1969:87-100) asked?

The conventional explanation of Chinese tenancy is that farmers mortgaged their farms during famines and, unable to repay, would yield the land to the lenders, staying on as renters. But if this were the only cause, tenancy would have developed heavily in the north, where famines were frequent. Why did it not?

In addressing this question, Perkins agreed with an earlier historian, Tawney (1932: 37), who found that farming in the north was so risky that northern peasants could not find lenders to feed their starving families. Therefore, they did not lose their farms.

"If conditions were hard enough," Perkins (1969:100) remarked, "they lost their lives instead."

In the south, however, where lands were more fertile, lenders could be found. Often they were other farmers, who would own one farm and assume another for debt, charging the former owner 30% to 40% of the crop as rent.

When Mao's armies executed thousands of landowners, his victims were not latifundistas living off the fat of their serfs. Typically, they were small farmers, each on three acres or so, eking out their own living, who had rescued their neighbors from starving but were making them repay through abusive rents. Was this a reason to execute them?

Did such a murderous beginning portend a just revolution?

Still, at one Yearly Meeting a Friend stated the view that since the Chinese had conquered famine, this alone made the revolution successful. But another Friend replied, "Taiwan also conquered famine. So did India and Korea."

Most Friends are aware that hybrid seeds of the green revolution conquered famine, not any particular government system. Experiments begun in the American Midwest in the 1950s leaped all national boundaries to feed increasing hundreds of millions in Asia.

However, many Friends seemed unaware that starvation and malnourishment have afflicted China in recent decades. The Chinese government itself has produced evidence that this is so.

It has also been documented by a British researcher (MacFarquhar 1974:197) and an American economist (Lardy 1983:152). MacFarquhar was a Labor Member of Parliament, who went to China to interview some who had lived through the Great Leap Forward of 1958 through 1960. The Chinese government made documents of the period available to him.

To diversify China, the government ordered farmers to build small steel mills in their back yards. But the steel was uneconomical and of poor quality. Coal, which should have been concentrated in larger mills in Manchuria, was hauled across the country in trains that should have hauled food.

The government forced farmers to operate the mills, even as tons of crops were rotting in the fields for want of harvesters. When a student from Mainland China, whom I asked to comment on the first draft of this chapter, saw the paragraph you have just read, he wrote me as follows:

> Since the Great Leap began in 1958, many local officials had complained about starving and poverty in the countryside. Peng Dehuai, a Chinese marshal, Minister of National Defense, went to the countryside to investigate and found that the complaints were true. He thought the central government must stop the Great Leap immediately.
>
> He wrote his investigation report to Mao. . . . Mao was very angry and dismissed him from all his highly important posts.

Foodgrain output dropped severely. The government blamed the poor harvest. But the harvest was not poor enough to explain why 1957 levels were not regained until the early 1970s.

MacFarquhar (p. 330) writes that . . .

> . . . for one *hsien* (county) in Kwangtung province was revealed during the cultural revolution: 20,000 people starved to death. Nationwide, the mortality rate doubled from 1.08 per cent in 1957 to 2.54 per cent in 1960. In that year the population actually *declined* by 4.5 per cent. Anywhere from 16.4 to 29.5 million extra people died during the leap, because of the leap.

The Great Leap Forward was such a disaster that Mao's power was temporarily eclipsed. He remained in the background during the early 1960s, while he mobilized his forces for a return to power.

Calling his opponents backsliders and "capitalist-roaders," he launched the Great Proletarian Cultural Revolution of 1967. He appealed to the young, the students, and the army.

Red Guards swept through government buildings and destroyed offices, furniture, and records. They burned university libraries. China possessed no government, no higher education, just mob rule.

Intellectuals were forced into the countryside to do penance working on farms. Government leaders were executed. One of the founders of the Revolution, Liu Shaoqi, a companion of Mao on the Great March, was purged and, many believe, assassinated.

Lardy (p. 159) observed that "China is probably the only country to combine, over twenty years, a doubling of real per capita income . . . and constant or even declining food consumption." In his final summary (pp. 186-7) he noted:

> The county-level data . . . suggest that absolute deprivation was widespread . . . Programs had not eliminated malnutrition and had left wide variations in the level of life expectancy . . . Government policy contributed to the immiseration of a significant portion of the peasantry.

After the death of Mao in 1976 and the ascendancy of Deng Xiaoping, the communes were dismantled by government fiat just as they had been formed.

Although not *owning* them, farmers were allotted "private" plots, part of whose output they may sell on the free market. The other part must be sold to the state, which pays for grain only 20% of the free market price (Tregarthen 1987:4).

With the free-market incentive, farm output immediately soared. The increase for six years, 1978-1984, was equal to that of the previous 29 years, 1949-1978.

In the period 1985-1987, however, the increase tapered off. One reason, Lardy suggested in an interview, is "the decline in government investment in agriculture . . . (and) with prices for farm goods still held artificially low by the Government and the costs of the manufactured goods needed in agriculture high, many peasants are choosing to go into industry, construction, or other work" (Butterfield 1987:E2).

They are also switching from grain to more profitable crops, which always happens when one price is held low and others are allowed to rise.

While this change augurs ill for feeding the Chinese people in the near future, at least they have choices they could not make under Mao.

Yet we are left with the question: Have the Chinese gained enough leverage on their government that it cannot reverse the liberalizing reforms of the 1970s?

Possibly. Every time history repeats itself, it does so a little differently. At some point it might reach a threshold.

But let us not accept the common confusion that the government of China *is* the people or even that it responds to the people's wishes.

Only if the people are strong enough to hold their government in check through local, indigenous institutions, will the dynastic cycle be broken. That has never happened before.

Chapter Four

Multinational Corporations

Why has anti-business, anti-profit sentiment grown in the Society of Friends? Why were
Friends of my third journey so upset about multinational corporations (MNCs)?

The conduct of the International Telephone
and Telegraph Company (ITT) in Chile was un-
doubtedly one of the reasons.

In 1970, when Salvador Allende was elected
President of Chile, ITT - in connivance with the
Central Intelligence Agency - considered all
means possible to prevent him from taking office, including bribery and military coup. If
all else failed, foreign companies and banks
would create chaos by refusing to extend technical
cal cooperation or by cutting off loans, thus
starving Chilean businesses financially. This
chaos would presumably bring about the coup.

ITT internal documents describing these
plans were leaked to Jack Anderson, columnist
for the *Washington Post,* who told his readers
about them. So far as I know, the documents were
not released in the United States.

But the Chilean government published them, and I bought a copy at a newsstand in Santiago. I have read the documents carefully, and when I compare them with news reports in the United States and lack of denials from ITT, I come to believe they are true.

Another reason for anti-business sentiment is the military support given by the U. S. government in 1954 to Guatemalan rightist forces who overthrew the reformist president, Jácobo Arbenz.

It is widely rumored, I believe correctly, that one of the considerations was that Arbenz would have conducted a land reform to confiscate, among others, the holdings of United Fruit Company.

Other incidents abound. Fruit-growing multinationals have grabbed lands from third-world peasants for their own plantations. Pharmaceutical companies have marketed drugs in the third world which were outlawed as dangerous in the United States. The Nestlé Company high-pressured mothers in the third world to abandon healthy breast-feeding.

I have two questions about MNCs. First, is such behavior characteristic of all MNCs? Second, do businesses other than MNCs behave in these ways?

Stereotypes about the behavior of ethnic groups usually collapse when subjected to these two questions. Might stereotypes of MNCs also fail upon close scrutiny?

The ITT documents indicate that when other MNCs were approached to join the "chaos" plan, they all refused. ". . . of all the companies involved," one of the smuggled ITT memos complained, "ours alone has been responsive and understood the problem."

Almost all Friends at my workshop at Friends General Conference knew about ITT's plot in Chile, but no one had heard about other MNCs *refusing* to join it.

Furthermore, to the extent that ITT-type behavior exists, I believe it is found in ordinary businesses, ordinary people, and governments, both in the third world and in the United States.

When behavior is general, it is inaccurate to attribute it specifically to one group, whether WASPS, Blacks, Jews, Quakers, or multinational corporations.

Multinational corporations have been charged with many sins: stealing land from peasants, overpaying their labor, underpaying their labor, using machines instead of labor, quashing unions, murdering union leaders, cheating on taxes, bribing governments, falsifying exports and imports, taking profits out of the country, racism, and more.

I heard all these charges during my third journey. I have no doubt they are sometimes true, since MNCs are run by people, and these are things that people sometimes do.

Wondering whether these charges were accurate representations, five years ago I read widely on MNCs. Then I wrote a chapter in Loehr and Powelson (1983), summarizing my findings.

For the most part, I found that multinational corporations do not earn a much greater rate of profit than do most businesses. They are usually not monopolies. Their officers are about as honest as ordinary citizens.

They pay their workers well. They negotiate with labor unions and do not quash them as a rule. Their officers are not murderers. And most of them don't steal land or bribe governments.

A study by the International Labor Organization (1973) showed that MNCs in the third world pay wages, on average, twice as high as local businesses and offer significantly more fringe benefits: housing, schools, hospitals and health services.

Arthur D. Little Company, an independent research organization monitoring MNCs in South Africa for the Sullivan Code, found them much more advanced than local companies in their attitudes toward black workers.

One of my workshops at Friends General Conference occurred just after another workshop, in which the speaker had shown how MNCs move to the third world where labor is cheap, leaving their ex-workers unemployed at home. Both seeking cheap labor and creating unemployment were wrong, this speaker felt. The subject was carried over to my meeting.

I shocked Friends by saying that I thought these moves were healthy if one took a *world* view rather than a parochial American one. Wages are low in the third world because so many workers are unemployed, mostly with malnourished families, some starving. Why is it wrong for a multinational corporation to offer them jobs?

"But what about the unemployed back home?" Friends protested.

"Back home," I replied, "we have one of the lowest rates of unemployment in the world, and year after year we create more new jobs than there are young people growing into employable age minus older people growing out of it."

Friends were incredulous, yet this is true. It is far, far easier for our own unemployed to find jobs than for workers in the third world. Also, many of our workers get unemployment insurance, whereas those of the third world starve.

Here was I, already accused by Friends of defending the rich, now defending the third-world poor against Friends who defended better-paid and socially protected Americans.

When Friends object to giving jobs at living wages to starving people, their feelings about multinational corporations must be strong indeed. Are Friends against certain kinds of behavior, or are Friends against multinational corporations?

Chapter Five

Nicaragua

At Friends General Conference at Oberlin, Nicaragua preoccupied a significant and earnest minority of participants at two workshops. Almost every topic that anyone mentioned would be interpreted to apply to Nicaragua. Nor could I communicate with this group without arousing hostility.

Why, I asked myself? This question brings me deep concern, and I continue to seek guidance.

In *Facing Social Revolution* I tried to put Nicaragua into a wider, third-world context. Not only Nicaragua, but many governments in the third world have confiscated land from an already-decaying aristocracy.

Instead of bestowing the benefits upon the poor, however, either they keep them for the state or they farm so inefficiently that there are no benefits. They tell the farmers what crops to plant and when and how to plant them. They require that some or all of the harvest be sold to state monopolies at prices specified by the state.

In addition, farmers must obtain their fertilizers, seeds, and credit from state monopolies, again at prices set by the state.

By squeezing the farmers, with high prices for inputs and low prices for outputs, governments force many to abandon the land to seek jobs in cities, which become overcrowded.

Food production has fallen in some countries, and many people are starving, mostly in Africa.

Nicaragua is one of many countries that has followed a variant of this pattern.

By contrast, those third-world countries that leave farming to the farmers, allowing them to select their own crops, sell where they will at whatever prices they can get, are the very ones that are most increasing food output per capita.

They are feeding their people better and improving the income and well-being of their poor. Not only are the farmers better off in these countries, but the cities are better fed as well, and at lower prices.

Friends wanted to know in which countries these favorable changes are occurring. Among others, they are Bangladesh, Bolivia, Chile, some states in India, Paraguay, South Korea, and Taiwan. China and the Soviet Union, which have switched over partially to free markets, have improved food production greatly.

One Friend asked why I was "against coop-eratives." She told how she and her neighbors had formed a food cooperative to get good food at lower prices and how, by cooperating to buy in larger scale, the farmers in her area ac-quired their inputs at lower prices.

I told her I am *for* cooperatives. In the cooperative movement in the United States, farm-ers or consumers band together for large-scale marketing advantages. Membership is voluntary, and the cooperative is governed by its members.

Almost always, this is not so in the third world. Instead, "cooperatives" are usually de-creed by the state. Farmers *must* join them, and they become the vehicle by which the state squeezes the farmer.

Farmers *must* sell their crops to the "cooperative," which in turn sells them to the state at low prices. Farmers *must* buy their inputs from the "cooperative," which gets them from the state at high prices.

They are not allowed to seek a better deal elsewhere or to form a different cooperative. This is a general model, with local modifica-tions, but it describes most of what are called "cooperatives" in the third world.

The early disputes between the Nicaraguan government and the Miskito Indians occurred be-cause Miskito cooperative farming did not fit the Sandinista pattern, and the government tried to change it forcibly (Powelson and Stock 1987:254).

A vocal minority at both workshops at Friends General Conference, however, felt that the Miskito experience was a "mistake," and for the most part, Nicaraguan cooperatives were different. "Farmers are not required to join cooperatives," they said. "Many farms are still privately owned."

True, small farmers may refuse to join cooperatives in Nicaragua. But if they do they will pay a higher rate of interest for credit, if indeed they can get credit at all. They will not be allowed to sell their crops as widely as those in cooperatives.

Private farms are mainly those of large sugar and cotton growers. They have been allowed to retain their land because of their expertise, which would be lost if they should emigrate. Their export crops generate foreign exchange for the state. So they too must sell to the state at prices set by the state.

"Isn't the hunger in Nicaragua caused by the Contras?" Friends rejoined. "How can you expect farm output to increase if fields are destroyed and farmers killed? And how can they get the fertilizers and other inputs when the United States, their main supplier, boycotts them?"

Voices were high-pitched and the atmosphere not very Friendly. Why, I wondered, could we not discuss divergent views without animosity arising?

I had asserted my pacifism many times. I am *against* funding the Contras, whose actions are *barbaric.* I cannot find adjectives strong enough. I am *against* the war. I am *against* U.S. intervention. I accept that war has hurt Nicaraguan farming and that it is a principal cause of mass hunger, just as war also is in Angola, Mozambique, and Ethiopia.

But why did my assertions that hunger is multi-caused, that price and procurement policies in Nicaragua are the very same that have brought hunger in places where there are no wars, and that war and policies may *both* be at fault - why, I wondered, did these assertions meet such hostility? Were they not possibilities worthy of consideration and reflection?

I asked Friends to look at Tanzania as a possible guide to how Nicaragua might look 20 years from now without U.S. intervention.

After independence in 1963, Tanzanian farm output was increasing yearly. Beginning in 1967, President Nyerere ordered all farmers to join cooperatives (*Ujamaa* villages), so that the government might better serve them with electricity, water, schools, and hospitals, as well as seed and fertilizer. They were ordered to farm collectively, buying their inputs from, and selling their output to, state monopolies.

The Ruvumu Development Association, a voluntary cooperative in which President Nyerere once took a personal interest, was forcibly closed because its members would not conform to the state model for *Ujamaa* villages (Powelson and Stock 1987:52).

Refusing to move to the collectives, the Tanzanian farmers were forced to do so by the army. They ran away, back to their native huts in the country. The army fetched them and this time burned their huts.

Many farmers ran away to the cities. Farm output per capita began to decline in precisely the year the collectives were formed, and it remained consistently low for 20 years.

Only in 1987, when pushed to do so by the International Monetary Fund, did the Tanzanian government allow farmers to market their products more freely and to charge higher prices (Davidson 1988). For the first time in recent years, Tanzanian per capita income increased.

Most of what happened in Tanzania has had its counterpart in Nicaragua, including the forced movement of farmers, mostly Indians but also others.

Friends listened but said nothing. I could not tell how they felt about Tanzania, but no minds had been changed about Nicaragua.

"Don't you have anything good to say for Nicaragua?" one Friend asked.

The question startled me, for I realized I had dwelt on the negative. Yet it was not easy, because everything good that I can think of in an authoritarian state is qualified by its being authoritarian.

The finest thing in Nicaragua is probably the enthusiasm of youth, who have pitched in and worked hard for the revolution. But the qualification is whether they are on a "high" which will inevitably give way to a "low." Does permanent social change arise out of a pitch of excitement, or does it come about with calm acceptance of a long-term task?

I am delighted with the campaign for literacy and education, but I am disturbed that the new sentences learned are ones of hate for "enemies."

I am happy with the greater health care offered, yet I am aware that hospital walls display political slogans.

I wonder what I would do if my children were starving and unlettered, and suddenly they were offered food and learning, but only if they would take courses indoctrinating them into the Republican (or Democratic) Party and would sing the praises of Democratic (or Republican) presidents?

I am happy that young Americans go to Nicaragua to build schools and day-care centers and bring in the crops, but I am disturbed that they return endorsing the authoritarian state. Cannot Friends distinguish between doing good things in a village and supporting the national politics?

In a non-authoritarian society, "goods" and "bads" can be separated. A democracy can throw out one and keep the other. But in an authoritarian society they are fused. All action, good or bad, becomes political.

Some Friends accepted the Sandinista explanation that their leadership made a "mistake" when it killed or resettled the Miskito Indians, burning their homes. For two reasons I believe the Sandinista apology for this atrocity was strategic rather than moral.

The first is that similar abuse is common to "popular" revolutions, including those of Cuba, China, France, Mexico, and Russia. It was even repeated in Nicaragua after the government had apologized the first time, just as also occurred in Tanzania. Non-Indian peasants in Nicaragua were ordered to abandon their farms and livelihoods in combat zones, without any choice and, for many, against their will.

The second is that oppression is like child abuse. It perpetuates itself, generation unto generation. Paulo Freire, Brazilian revolutionary author, was aware of this. In *The Pedagogy of the Oppressed,* he showed how the oppressed may themselves become oppressors when they achieve power.

Jim Corbett, well known for his work on Sanctuary, has long been thinking on similar lines to my own. In a paper he prepared for a seminar at the Quaker conference center, Ben Lomond, in April 1987, he wrote:

If solidarity with the people of El Salvador, Guatemala, or Nicaragua means recognition that our common humanity transcends our separate national identities, that we here in the United States are morally responsible for our government's sponsorship of torture and murder in those countries, and that we must therefore exercise civil initiative to stop our government's criminal activities and protect the victims, *that is 180 degrees away from solidarity with a politico-military movement that claims to be the way to end oppression by means of revolutionary warfare.* (Italics added).

To Jim as to me, supporting revolutionary war as a means of ending oppression is inconsistent with our acceptance of a moral responsibility to stop our government's criminal actions and to hold to Friends' testimony for nonviolence.

Chapter Six

United States Policy

Foreign policy of the United States lay heavy on the minds of Friends in my third journey.

U.S. policy toward the third world appears to me to be based on two cardinal principles: keep the Soviet Union out, and keep "things" quiet: no riot, no revolution, no threat of either. In case of conflict between these principles, the first dominates the second. I think this has been our policy for more than 50 years.

Friends on my third journey seemed to agree. But many found other guiding principles, such as protecting multinational corporations, reinforcing dictators and landowners, obtaining raw materials at low prices for our industries, and expanding our industrial presence abroad.

But I thought the more important question was what priority these additional objectives assume. What would we do if protecting multinationals or dictators created conditions favorable to Soviet influence in Country X? Suppose protecting landowners would upset the quiet? What then?

- 68 -

Some Friends felt the contradiction would not arise, for protecting multinationals and anti-communism went together. Some thought our government considers dictators to be the best protection against communism always. A few thought we would oppose land reform under any circumstances, because we considered it "communist."

Fortunately, history sheds some light on these questions. In the first quarter of this century, the U.S. Government clearly protected multinationals. Multinationals supported the governments of host countries financially. Landowners and dictators bolstered those "friendly" governments.

In Venezuela, Dictator Gomez invited the oil companies to write the petroleum legislation in 1918. He and they divided the spoils, leaving only subsistence for the workers. Landowners, whose fortunes depended on poorly paid labor, supported that government. So did the hacienda Church.

Similar things can be said about copper in Chile, tin in Bolivia, timber in Paraguay, and iron and timber in Liberia.

The policies of European governments in Africa and Asia were similar, except that they installed colonial regimes where we relied on political relations.

When our policies changed, it was not because our government had acquired a moral sense. Rather, in the second quarter of this century interests shifted, and the facets that were once bound together began to conflict.

In the first quarter of this century, for example, we found it "necessary" to intervene in Cuba to prevent "unquiet." But certain political forces on that island found it to their interests to foment "unquiet" because they, being our government's favorites, would be put into power to quell what they had started.

Sergeant Batista gained control that way. Franklin Roosevelt, while supporting him because he thought he had to, was still aware that Batista was playing us for patsy.

Intervention in the Dominican Republic, which put Trujillo into power, and in Nicaragua, which pitted us against Sandino and in favor of Somoza, were for the same purpose.

All these despots created "unquiet" so the United States would call upon them to limit the forces they had unleashed.

These events shaped Roosevelt's thinking when he formed the Good Neighbor Policy in 1933. Never again, he said, would U.S. forces invade Latin America, a pledge that our government kept until the invasion of the Dominican Republic in 1965.

Furthermore, Roosevelt had begun to change our government's attitude toward multinationals. Previously, we had favored them because we believed they spread "our" system of private enterprise and democracy.

But as World War II approached, Mexico was nationalizing U.S. oil companies. Needing Mexico's friendship for the war, Roosevelt told the companies to make the best settlement they could. The U.S. Government would take no unusual measures to support them.

After World War II, the conflicts widened. Fighting the cold war against the Soviet Union, we needed allies in the third world. Yet governments there were nationalizing our multinationals.

Our protection for MNCs would have angered those governments, making them more likely to side with the Soviet Union. So we laid low. Public utilities and railroads all over the third world were expropriated, without response by Europeans or Americans.

The revolutionary Government of Bolivia nationalized the tin mines and expropriated the land in 1953-54. Not only did the United States not respond, but within a few years, when the Bolivian government was threatened by fiscal disaster ("unquiet"), we provided funds and economic advice to shore it up. I was the U.S. economic advisor to Bolivia in 1959-60.

We even supported Bolivia's land reform, supplying credit and advisors to the small farmers to whom the land had been given.

Mexico nationalized the electric power industry in the early 1960s, and our government did nothing.

Oil companies were the next target. One after another, they were nationalized in Venezuela, Peru, Indonesia, and the Middle East.

While writing an article on Peru after the nationalization of 1968, I interviewed the U.S. executive director for the International Monetary Fund (IMF) and the negotiator whom the President had appointed to assist the oil company.

Both the IMF director and the President's negotiator agreed that Peru had the right to nationalize the company, but both insisted on compensation. The IMF director said he would not approve any loans to Peru until the matter was settled.

Later on, compensation was agreed at an amount considerably less than the value of the company's property. My guess is that our government told the companies to "take it and run." Anyway, that is what they did.

Virtually the same happened when President Frei nationalized the copper companies in Chile in 1966-67. Compensation far less than full value was agreed, and the companies "took it and ran." Thereafter, the Frei government received much aid from the United States and was held up as a showcase for democracy.

Why, despite its nationalization of important U.S. companies? Because the United States wanted to keep Salvador Allende from being elected. We feared he would support the Soviets.

Once again, the multinationals were bested by our anti-Soviet interest.

It has been the same with land. Where once the landowners stood behind the dictators who stood behind the multinationals that stood behind stability and "our" way of life, by the end of World War II the landowners were no longer a force.

A new urban business group believed that feudal landlords retarded efficient food supply for urban workers. Both government and business were veering toward land reform.

The U.S. government responded to the new circumstances. Not out of concern for the poor peasant. Not out of a moral sense of justice. Our government responded because it was politically astute to do so.

Not only did we assist the land reform in Bolivia, but also land reforms all over the third world. We mandated land reform in Japan after World War II and laid it on heavily in South Korea and Taiwan. We wanted to break the hold of Japanese landowners, whom we considered a bulwark of the military classes in their country. They had held lands in Korea and Taiwan as well. We were in competition with the communists, and land reform was the tool.

If we no longer support multinationals or landowners, how about the dictators? The story is the same.

So long as dictators buttressed us against the Soviet Union and created "stability," we financed them, equipped their armies, and stood by them politically. But when the showdown came between anti-sovietism and the dictators, the dictators were the ones to go.

So it was with Pérez Jimenez in Venezuela. When he created more instability than stability, his time had come. We welcomed his removal from Caracas and found him refuge in the United States.

Out of sympathy for him? Hardly. When the Venezuelans extradited him for trial and imprisonment, we willingly handed him back.

So also with Somoza of Nicaragua, Baby Doc Duvalier of Haiti, and Marcos of the Philippines. So long as they served us, we served them.

But once their legitimacy was lost at home, and their further tenure would create "unquiet," we removed them as "quietly" as possible. At the time of writing, General Noriega in Panama is weakening, and the United States has indicted him for drug smuggling. If he were to set foot in our country, he would be arrested and tried.

So also with General Stroessner in Paraguay. Two years ago I spoke before the Paraguayan Economics Association in Asunción. The day before my courtesy call to the U.S. Ambassador, the Stroessner Government had closed down the opposition newspaper, *A.B.C. Color.*

I found the Ambassador furious. "The very morning they did it," he fumed, "I had been in the office of a cabinet minister who assured me that *A.B.C. Color* would not be closed. He lied to me! He lied to me! I have communicated with Washington, and they agree that we must protest in the strongest form." I feel sure the Ambassador was not putting on an act.

Later I asked the Political Officer at the Embassy how strong the opposition was. "Do you want to meet them?" he asked.

That evening he took me to the Catholic University. For several hours, with the Political Officer present, I talked with students, faculty, and others who are the ones who will some day overthrow the general or his successor.

At all times they were friendly with the Political Officer and with me, and always they sounded as if the United States was on their side. "Why do you keep in touch with the opposition?" I asked the Political Officer later. "We keep our options open," he replied.

These experiences, some personal, some from the media, some from economics articles, some from history books, and some from knowledgeable and sincere people, have shaped my belief on how U.S. policy functions toward the third world.

Events have overtaken the days when the United States would routinely support multinational corporations, landowners, and dictators. These forces first yielded their priorities to anti-Sovietism and keeping things quiet. Then they gradually slipped out of the picture.

But that picture is not a pretty one. Anti-sovietism, or anti-anything, does not make an innovative, far-thinking nation. Nor does trying to keep things "quiet," a policy not to be confused with pacifism.

Chapter Seven

The Rich Are Richer . . .
The Poor Are Poorer

In *Facing Social Revolution* (page 91), I wrote:

> From the end of the nineteenth century on, the ownership of wealth and income in England and the United States has [become] . . . more widespread and much less concentrated. This move toward greater equality has been strong but not continuous. There have been setbacks, such as an alarming one in the past decade. But we have always returned to the trend.

Some Friends were not comfortable with that statement. First, they doubted it. "Are not the rich getting richer and the poor getting poorer?"

Second, they thought I had paid short shrift to the setback of the past decade. What made me think that would be reversed, they asked?

For the past twelve years, a few of the already rich have become richer and some of the already poor poorer. But mostly the change has been an outflow from the middle classes. Some middle-income people have become richer and some poorer, so that *relatively,* there are more rich, more poor, and fewer left in the middle.

Those people you see on the ski slopes, paying over $100 a day for lift tickets for their families, or eating in fancy restaurants, are among the upwardly mobile, many with incomes of $50,000 or higher. Others, predominantly black, have slipped to $10,000 or less.

Let us put the change into historical perspective, first from the nineteenth century and then from today.

When I speak of "real" income, I mean inflation-adjusted: the goods that money income will buy. If money income goes up 15% but prices increase 5%, then real income is up 10%.

"Absolute" income is the same as real income, but this term contrasts with "relative" income, or percentage share. If A earns $100 and so does B, then A earns 50% of the incomes of both. If A's income goes up to $120 but B's goes up to $130, then A's share of their total income drops to 48% (or 120/250). Thus one's relative income may fall while one's absolute income rises.

Many economists believe that from 1800 to 1870 the poor were becoming better off, both relatively and absolutely. Real wages were slowly rising, both absolutely and relatively to profits. Others argue that the evidence is faulty.

But economists are agreed on the century from 1870 to 1970. Let us divide national income roughly into three sectors: high, middle, and low. For that century, the *absolute* income of all three sectors was rising, while in *numbers* of people, both ends were flowing into the middle.

The poor were becoming richer both relatively and absolutely. The rich were becoming richer absolutely, but poorer relatively. Except for the great depression, this was a prosperous century for the United States.

The poor were set back during the 1930s. A depression always harms the poor more than it does the rich.

From World War II until 1976, however, the earlier trend returned: real incomes across the board increased, while in numbers of people the ends resumed their flow into the middle.

Beginning in 1976, the direction shifted. Measured by families, for the past twelve years the rich have been getting richer and the poor poorer, at least relatively, and maybe absolutely as well. What happened, Friends asked?

First, let's look at statistics. Table 1 shows the relative share in total income of the poorest fifth in the population, of the next-to-the-poorest fifth, the middle fifth, the next-to-the-richest fifth, and the richest. These five shares add to 100%.

A separate line shows the percentage of the richest 5%, which is part of the "highest fifth" shown above it.

As we would expect, the percentages increase as we move down each column, from poorest fifth to next-to-poorest, and on to the richest.

Now look at the top line, the relative share of income going to the poorest fifth of American families. It decreased between 1947 and 1950, but this movement - which I cannot explain - was contrary to trend.

In year-to-year comparison from 1947 to 1976, however, the relative share of the poor went up more than down, so that from 1947 (1950) until 1970 it increased from 5.0% (4.5%) to 5.4%, staying at approximately this level until 1976. (It was actually 5.5% in 1973 and 1974).

Thereafter it declined, and by 1985 (latest year for which we have data), the poorest fifth was receiving only 4.6% of the income.

Now look at the share going to the richest fifth.

Table 1
Income Shares in the United States,
selected years, 1947-1985.*
(Percentages)

1/5 population	1947	1950	1970	1976	1985
Poorest	5.0	4.5	5.4	5.4	4.6
Second	11.8	11.9	12.2	11.8	10.9
Third	17.0	17.4	17.6	17.6	16.9
Fourth	23.1	23.4	23.8	24.1	24.2
Richest	43.2	42.8	40.9	41.1	43.5
Top 5%	17.5	17.3	15.6	15.6	16.7

SOURCE: 1947,1950,1970, US Department of Commerce, *Historical Statistics of the United States*, vol. 1, Series G 31-138, p. 293.

1976: US Department of Commerce, *Statistical Abstract of the United States for 1978*, Table 734, p. 455.

1985: *Statistical Abstract* for 1987, Table 733, p. 437.

Data in three columns add to .1 above or below 100.0% because of rounding.

----

*Statistics such as these are suspect for any given year, since they are gathered by sample, and there may be sampling errors. When they show a pattern year after year, however, they gain credibility. Friends are wise to question tables of "selected years," since by selection one can often tell the story one chooses. But I have examined the data for all the years in between those shown, and they confirm the pattern.

In 1947, it had 43.2% of the income. From then until 1976, its share generally eroded, to 41.1%. While earning more absolutely, people in this fifth were losing relatively. Then the relative trend reversed itself and began to rise, to 43.5% in 1985. We see the same pattern for the top 5%.

Now look at the middle fifth.

In 1947 it had 17.0% of the income, and from then until 1976 its share gradually increased (always with a few year-to-year slight exceptions) to 17.6%. Thereafter, however, it dropped, to 16.9% in 1985.

All this means that in the postwar years until 1976, income inequality was being slowly reduced: the relative flow was out of both ends into the middle. Using data not on this table, we know that all groups were becoming richer absolutely.

But after 1976, the tendency changed. The poorest group got *less*, the richest group *more*, and there were fewer in the middle.

In 1986, there was a hint of reversal again, as the number of people below the poverty line dipped and the median family income rose (Pear 1987:A12). But this is one year only - we do not have data for 1987 yet - so until more information comes, I will not presume a re-reversal.

Why, suddenly after 1976, was the trend reversed? No one knows for sure. But there are some clues.

The data show percentages of families, not of people, in each bracket. Since 1947, the number of families has increased by approximately 1.5% per year and by about 2.1% for Blacks, compared to an increase in the over-all population by 1.3% per year (down to 0.9% in recent years). The percentage increase in families is greater than the percentage increase in people because of the formation of baby-boom families and the splitting of families because of divorce.

As couples divorce, the new families are probably poorer than the average of the old. The two new families cannot each maintain the income of the previous, integral family.

In an opposite move, families staying together but shifting from one income to two move into higher brackets.

These opposing changes increase the disparity among families.

Why are the poor getting poorer? To answer this, we must find out who are the poor.

They are very largely black families in urban ghettos, headed by women, with large numbers of children, many out of wedlock. While there are more white families in poverty than black, nevertheless the black group accounts for the major increase since 1976.

Why has this happened, and why now?

Daniel Moynihan postulated that it was a heritage of slavery. This explanation is probably not correct, because black families showed great stability (few divorces, few out-of-wedlock children) for the first hundred years after slavery had ended.

Others suggest the trend is a result of present and persistent discrimination.

But we had the same or more discrimination earlier. So discrimination cannot explain the *changes* of the 1970s: why urban black families have been increasingly headed by single women; why more children have been born out of wedlock; why more young males have dropped out of school; and why Blacks have become more concentrated in urban ghettos.

Studies done by both black and white social scientists and by government commissions have suggested reasons - all speculative - which include the following:

1. Technological improvement has upgraded the skills needed for jobs, and young Blacks have not increased their capabilities proportionately. But this "answer" only asks another question: Why not?

2. With the mechanization of southern farming, displaced black workers have migrated to northern ghettos. This must be part of the reason but cannot be all of it.

3. Many new jobs created in the past decade have been filled by women not previously in the work force, at the expense of black men. Again this may be part of the reason, but the magnitudes are not great enough to explain it all.

4. The trends among Blacks are part of a national trend. There are more out-of-wedlock births, more divorces, and more female-headed families among Whites too.

However, the increased proportions of all of these have been greater for Blacks than for Whites, and surely urban Blacks have been less able to cope with such difficult family situations. Therefore, a *national* problem has affected Blacks more proportionately than Whites. Why?

5. While discrimination is a cause, again it is not an adequate explanation. Despite discrimination, many Blacks have moved upward. Not only have they *not* dropped out of school, but many have gone on to college and graduate school, becoming professionals.

Thus Blacks show the same demographic and income trends as the total population: out of the middle, both up and down. What determines whether a person will go up or down?

6. The upwardly-mobile Blacks moved out of the ghetto. When Blacks *had* to live together, because housing discrimination was legal and usual, those upwardly-mobile served as role-models.

Now that they have gone, the remaining young males are peer-pressured into street gangs and dead ends.

Responding to affirmative action, employers drain off the yuppie Blacks, leaving the rest all the more isolated.

In this explanation, *both* nondiscrimination in housing and affirmative action have unintended, negative consequences. But this does not mean these policies should be abandoned. Perhaps they should be intensified.

All the above, both the explanations and doubts about them, are found in the studies. No part is original with me, and I offer no judgments on their accuracy. So why do I even mention them?

Because in my third journey, I was told by many Friends that "capitalism" and "discrimination" are the root causes of poverty. "Unemployment and poverty are ingrained in our system," some insisted.

But the great improvements in the nineteenth century and up until 1976, as well as the upward mobility for some Blacks since then, would suggest that capitalism scarcely merits the scorn that some Friends heap upon it.

More importantly, I fear that generalized stereotypes will not direct us toward educated action.

I urge Friends to pinpoint poverty in specific families, in the backgrounds and burdens of real persons - Sally, Joe, Millie, whomever. Let us examine the reasons for their unemployment or lack of education, in the environment both inside and outside the home, including job discrimination, in television, drugs, and peer pressures in desperate neighborhoods.

It is futile to assign blame, "theirs" or "ours." Instead, let us define what the poor can do to help themselves and then seek ways by which the non-poor can help them, individually, collectively through churches or other agencies, or through government.

We need not await a full understanding of the causes before helping individuals, person by person, neighborhood by neighborhood.

Has your Meeting or Church considered the extent and root causes of poverty? Have you identified poverty in your neighborhood or your city? Have you taken action both to relieve suffering and to attack the cause?

Chapter Eight

"I Am Rich
Because They are Poor"

"I am poor because you are rich." So said President Julius Nyerere of Tanzania before the United Nations in 1975.

Nyerere's echo is heard among Friends who believe that our wealth rests on the poverty of others, that we eat cheap bananas for example, because fruit companies steal land from third-world farmers.

Many times during my third journey I heard the belief that "we are rich because they are poor."

Yet all my training in economics, all my reading in history, and all my experience in some fifty countries of the third world, tell me this is not so.

I do not deny that companies steal land from the poor with the connivance of despotic governments. The work of a third-world farmer is cruel, dirty, long, and poorly paid.

Tourists buy handicrafts cheaply in Mexican markets because sellers earn little. The paltry sum we pay for pineapples and bananas leaves little for the farmers who grew them.

But turn these sentences around - reverse the causation - and they cease to be true.

If the world were rid of despotic governments and land could no longer be stolen; if the work of third-world farmers were cleaner and less cruel; if they were better paid; if hours were shorter, *our bananas and pineapples would be even cheaper, not more costly,* as I will explain below.

Poverty in three fourths of the world harms everyone, rich and poor. If the poor earned more, both we and they would be richer.

The logic of this is seen in the industrialized world - North America, Europe, Australia, New Zealand, Japan - where high wages are paid while goods are produced cheaply. Our best trade, a source of our wealth, is with other industrialized countries, not with the third world.

We are rich because we buy cheap automobiles and stereo sets from Japan, cheap watches from Switzerland, cheap cameras from West Germany, and cheap food from our own country. These may seem expensive because of our inflation, but they are cheap in labor terms. Over the years, wages have gone up more than prices.

This is true for all these regions. Japanese wages now rival those in several European countries.

Cheap pineapples from the Philippines and cheap bananas from Central America are but a pittance in our budget. Double or triple what we pay for them or conversely give them to us free, and we would scarcely feel the difference.

Nor do most of our primary products - products of the soil, such as minerals and foods - come from the third world, as is sometimes believed. Most come from industrialized nations.

Instead, wealth is gained by technology, good business management, entrepreneurship and innovation, not by gouging a few pesos off the prices of pineapples and bananas.

"But," Friends persisted, "if pineapples and bananas are but a pittance in our budget, still they are a large part of third-world income. Why don't we pay more, when it means so much to them and so little to us?"

Suppose we did pay more for bananas in Central America. Would the banana picker receive more? Not likely, because banana-picker wages depend not on the price of bananas but on other wages in the region. The extra price would go into banana company profits.

Furthermore, since a higher price would cause some consumers to eat other fruits instead of bananas, fewer pickers would be needed. Not only would we not raise wages, but we would cause a few pickers to be fired.

For other ways in which well-intentioned actions to help the poor may harm them instead, see my Pendle Hill pamphlet, *Holistic Economics.*

How, then, do we help raise wages in the third world?

First, we ask: how have wages risen, from time immemorial, all over the world? The answer: by increased productivity of labor. This means that one worker, in any occupation, produces more than he or she did before.

This may happen in numerous ways: A machine makes the worker turn out goods faster. A new management technique (say, reorganizing the product flow in a factory) leads to more goods from the same number of workers. Or a new product is more valued in the market.

It does not matter in which activity productivity increases. If worker productivity goes up in cotton, the wages of banana pickers will also rise. Why? As wages in cotton go up, unless banana companies equal them their workers will abandon bananas to pick cotton.

Not only will all wages rise when productivity increases, but the prices of the goods affected will fall.

I mean "real" prices. If cotton sells for $10 a bale and $10 buys a watch, then the real price of a bale of cotton is one watch, or any other good similarly calculated. We use real prices to ignore inflation. If both cotton and the watch go to $20, then the real price of each is unchanged.

Let me summarize: an increase in the productivity of cotton workers increases the real wages of both cotton and banana pickers, while also reducing the real price of cotton.*

Extend these principles to all products, and we have the formula for overcoming poverty. How to implement it is the unresolved question.

Thus, instead of offering to pay more for bananas, let us think of ways to increase production per worker in cotton or any other third-world goods. Labor productivity is indeed increasing in the so-called newly-industrializing countries: South Korea, Taiwan, Hong Kong, and Singapore. So also in Japan for decades and in Europe, North America, New Zealand and Australia for centuries.

There is much scope for it yet to happen in the third world. Friends would do well to seek ways to broaden that scope rather than to increase prices within a narrower scope.

----

*There may be some exceptions. The exact proportions for wages in cotton versus wages in bananas and for wages versus prices vary according to circumstance. Economists know about the exceptions, and we have ways to estimate the proportions. I tell you this only so that my colleagues will not jump on me for being too simple. But the economics lesson has gone far enough. It tells the probable results, and I will not complicate it further.

Chapter Nine

Russia and its Revolution

If China's revolution recurred many times, what about that of Russia? Did the revolutions of 1917 also re-initiate an historic cycle, which, if it runs its course, will leave the citizens where they were before?

I believe that unlike China, *Russia has never had a revolution.* Russian citizens have about the same economic and political rights as they did in the sixteenth century, to wit:

> All Russian citizens belonged to some noble or tsar. What they produced belonged to their over-lords, who let them keep a portion on which to live. They were not al-lowed to move from place to place nor to leave the country without permission, nor might they take an occupation of their choice.

Substitute "government" for "noble or tsar," and this description applies today.

In many ways, the welfare of Russians has improved. The government is less cruel. It no longer kills or tortures its citizens on whim, though it imprisons them or puts them into mental hospitals. People eat and live better. They have more education, health services, and housing.

In none of these arenas, however, does the Soviet Union equal the West. In principle, it supplies these services more equitably than does the West. In practice, availability is scant and quality poor outside work places of strategic interest to the government.

Why is the Soviet Union so far behind the West, economically and materially? Soviets often point to the numerous encirclements and invasions, by the Mongols, the Turks, western Europeans, and yes, the United States in 1918.

But none of these makes Russia peculiar, for they all occurred in a world where invasion was the norm. During the centuries when Russia was encircled and invaded, the following events also took place:

France invaded Germany and Germany France. Both gobbled up Burgundy and the Low Countries. English armies were in France for over a century, except for periodic truces. Prussia absorbed other German states.

France, England, and Spain fought over the Netherlands. Sweden overwhelmed northern Germany and Poland. Austria, France, and Spain vied for Italy. Poland was divided among Prussia, Russia, and Austria.

Furthermore, the Russians have invaded more territories, east and west and south of them, than they ever lost through invasion. In most of these, they are still there. No, encirclement does not explain Russian backwardness.

So, what does?

I believe that material progress, for both rich and poor, depends on the free interchange of ideas and the free movement of people, goods, and capital.

It depends on the dilution of monopolies, whether of government, military, feudal or private business, so they do not harass people, tax them unduly, prevent them from moving or force them to move, or underpay their labor or overcharge them for products.

These conditions grew slowly in western Europe and Japan through patient bargaining, conflict resolution, and compromise. They are still growing, for no nation has reached perfection.

But they are hard to perceive in the Soviet Union and China, and I do not detect them at all in most of the third world.

In the fifteenth and sixteenth centuries in Russia, the tsar and nobles tightened control over their domains. Little by little the peasants lost their freedom.

First, they were allowed to move only on certain days of the year, later not at all. Greater amounts of forced services and taxes were inflicted. By the end of the sixteenth century they were serfs in fact, if free in name.

Westerners usually think of feudalism and serfdom as being "medieval," stemming from the dark ages and abolished about the sixteenth century. But the enserfment in Russia of that century also happened to farmers all over eastern Europe, and they did not become juridically free until the nineteenth century.

Thus peasants were being enserfed in the East at the very time they were being emancipated in the West.

In the West, serfs had bargained for their freedom little by little. At one time they were allowed to move. At another they paid cash rent for land instead of services. At still another they were confirmed as owners.

One time they were freed from one service, another time from another. When the French revolution abolished remaining feudal dues in 1789, there were only a few left.

When Peter the Great of Russia visited the West in 1697-98, he marveled at Dutch and English science and industry, which he thought were the secret of economic advance.

But he completely missed the point that Western workers were free and wage-earning. When he ordered new factories to be built in Russia, he copied Western technology, but state serfs built them and state serfs worked in them.

Three centuries later, Russia has yet to catch up with Western industry.

Economic historians usually put the free farmer-serf boundary in the sixteenth to nineteenth centuries at the Elbe River in Germany, while admitting that the "line" was really a broad swath.

A traveler from France to Russia in those centuries would have found peasants less and less free the farther east he or she went.

The Habsburgs of Austria-Bohemia-Hungary considered all families to be part of the royal corporation. Where one worked, what one did, how much one paid in rents and taxes, even marriages could be decreed by the nobility or the royal court. Maria Theresa and her son, Joseph II, tried to free the peasants by fiat, but their efforts were reversed after Joseph died in 1790.

As late as in the 1890s, German intellectuals were debating whether peasants on the east German estates should be allowed to move or marry without permission of the estate owner.

Russian tsar and nobles did not rule peasant family life the way the Habsburgs and the Prussians did, but they ruled all economic activity.

Our traveler would also have found farming less and less productive the farther east he or she went: poorer seeds, less use of fertilizer, less modern practices, all resulting in lower yield per hectare. The lesson was clear: serf labor produces less than free.

Today the Elbe River marks part of the boundary between western and eastern Europe, which Winston Churchill dubbed the "iron curtain."

Most observers consider this a machination of the twentieth century. But the cleavage is much older.

Only in the nineteenth century did rulers in the East become aware of how backward their principalities were. Napoleon brought them not only Western ideas of humanism but also farm organization and technology. They learned that an unfree peasantry causes backwardness, which in turn helped explain why they lost wars.

Emancipation decrees became fashionable, in Poland and Prussia in 1807, Hesse in 1820, Saxony in 1832, Austria in 1848, and Hungary in 1853.

Russia was next to last. In 1861, shocked by the loss of the Crimean War, importuned by industrialists, cajoled by intellectuals, but opposed by nobles, Tsar Alexander II decreed peasant freedom. Only Romania came later, in 1864.

All told, thirty-nine European nations and principalities freed their serfs from 1771 to 1864. Mostly, these were in the East.

Yet the Russian serf was still not free. He had to buy his land, at 80% of the value, with money loaned by the government, repayable over 49 years at 6% interest. The burden was so great that most peasants scratched hard to subsist.

Even after he had paid for it, the peasant's land was subject to the authority of the village *(mir).* A passport was required to leave.

But a peasant who preferred a factory job would not be issued a passport until he had paid his debt for the land, and even so only with permission of the village officials and the father of his household.

The village official would refuse if the peasant was needed at home. The father would often refuse because the family's land allotment would be reduced if a member were away.

Not surprisingly, agricultural output did not increase much, and peasant poverty persisted. In the 1870s, protesters known as *Narodniki* (from *narod,* people) tried to organize peasants but failed.

Only extreme agricultural retardation moved Tsar Nicholas II to call a special conference in 1901, which decided that outmoded structures, especially the village, were the chief reason for backwardness. Loss of a war to Japan in 1905 jolted the government further.

In the so-called Stolypin Reforms, dictated from above, peasants were allowed to convert village holdings into private property under certain conditions. But they quarreled over who owned what, and only about 10% of the lands had been processed before the revolutions of 1917.

Although the government abolished private landholding after the October revolution, peasants seized most of the farmland and treated it as if it were theirs. By 1919, 96.8% of cultivable land was held by peasants (Atkinson 1983:182).

Eager for industrial development just as governments of the third world are today, the Soviets did what third-world governments are now doing. To move food from farm to city, they did not allow thousands of independent farmers to sell directly to city markets. Instead, they declared the government to be monopoly buyer of grain and set the prices low.

The farmers responded just as third-world farmers are responding today: by consuming as much as they could, delivering as little as possible to the government, and selling in the black market.

Some abandoned the farm. Instead of cooperating as they might have, the political leaders and the farmers became locked in a struggle for grain.

After the death of Lenin, a great debate ensued on how to extract food from the peasants. All agreed that the peasant would have to pay for Soviet industrialization by supplying grain to the cities.

Preobrazhensky argued that the extraction would have to be even more severe than under the tsar, while Trotsky thought the city worker would also sacrifice by accepting low wages.

Bukharin believed that in the spirit of revolution peasants would allow themselves to be taxed. Therefore they should be left in private ownership of farms, which they would decide voluntarily to collectivize.

These three men, it seems to me, were paternalizing both the peasant and the city worker, by deciding in their executive forums how each would react, without consulting either. Third-world governments are repeating this paternalistic behavior today.

Stalin at first took the moderate side, that of Bukharin, using it to denounce his opponents and consolidate his power. In 1928 he reversed himself, swinging over to Preobrazhensky's position on rapid collectivization. He fired Bukharin from the Comintern and executed him in 1938. (Bukharin was cleared in 1988 by a Party commission reviewing purge trials).

Stalin collectivized at gunpoint. In one swift decree, the village commune *(mir)* - a tradition of centuries - was wiped out. Armed mobs were sent from the cities.

Peasants resisted *en masse.* Farms in the Ukrainian grain belt were overrun and destroyed.

Estimates of the dead vary. Some were killed outright, but many died of human-made famine. Robert Conquest (1986), who studied Soviet archives and other sources, puts the total dead at about 14.5 million.

Only state-run collectives and state farms were left. If the subsequent Stalin purges are also included, Conquest estimates, about 20 million Soviet citizens lost their lives.

Once again, however, the government had to confront the lesson that is still unlearned by so many, even today. Ordering peasants to grow grain does not make them do it. Farm output, already decimated by violent collectivization, fell by about 25% more during the first Five-Year Plan (1929-1934). Forced procurement, however, doubled the supply of food to the cities. Stalin's urban workers won, while peasants starved.

By the late 1950s, the collectives averaged 5,000 acres and 200 families. Peasants received their orders from the authorities, who compensated them on the basis of work units. Government took most of the output to distribute in the cities. Little was left for peasants.

Suspecting that incentives might work better than force, Khrushchev quintupled farmers' wages from 1953 to 1958. The Kosygin/Brezhnev administration increased both wages and farm prices further in 1964, and the government invested more in agriculture and supplied more fertilizer. Immediately, output increased, by

3.9 per cent a year from 1950 to 1970 (Johnson and Brooks 1983:12).

From 1970 to 1979, however, growth of food output slowed to 1.2 per cent per year (Johnson and Brooks 1983:12). When three decades are taken together, the performance of Soviet agriculture is respectable, compared with annual increases of about 2.0 per cent in the United States and 2.2 per cent in Europe. But slow growth in the 1970s and 1980s is worrisome. Most outside observers believe Soviet agriculture is inefficient and wasteful of labor.

The Soviets do lead in those industries where the government can command, such as in space vehicles. They produce efficient steel.

But they lag where central control is difficult to enforce, as in manufacturing consumer goods. Their people do not have enough houses. It will be years, possibly decades, before families have a standard of living equal to that of the West.

In the early 1980s, there were a few signs that the lesson of the ages would at last be learned. After they have performed their duties to the collectives, Soviet farmers are now allowed to grow what they wish on small plots and to sell in free markets. This is not land they own, but land they may use.

Although these plots are only about 3% of land sown, they grow over 15% of farm output. About one third of Soviet meat and milk, two thirds of potatoes and two fifths of fruits and vegetables come from "private" plots (Johnson and Brooks 1983:6).

Overall, agricultural output has increased by 1.5% per year, from 1979 to 1985 (FAO 1987:90).

This liberalization has been expanded with *glasnost,* Gorbachev's program for replacing Soviet controls. Some political prisoners have been released and some Jews allowed to emigrate. Means of expression, including art and religion, have become freer. The Yeltsin affair of 1987 even brought verbal mass protests.

But the main lines of agricultural policy remain unchanged. The government still cannot bring itself to trust the farmer. It still watches closely over the minutest operation details: crop areas, plowing dates and rates of seeding, harvesting, delivery quotas, and the annual and five-year plans for each farm.

Like other Soviet citizens, the peasant may still not move without police permission. Outside his small "private" plot he has nothing to say about agricultural practices. In these respects, little has changed since the sixteenth century.

When I relate these facts to Friends, the response is sometimes grim. "Why do you say these bad things?" they ask. "Are you not compounding the misunderstanding that already divides us from the Soviets?

"Are you not confirming what our President says, that Russia is the Evil Empire?* Are you not making war more likely?"

I do not think so. I think ignorance, not truth, makes war more likely.

Some Friends of my third journey thought of collective farms as arising out of people whose love, cooperation, and compassion are more advanced than those of "profit-seeking" farm corporations in our own country.

But we do not need to minimize the authoritarian state. It is not authoritarian state versus democracy that causes war. Instead, it is the fear the two nations have of each other.

We do not achieve peace by convincing ourselves that the Soviet Union is less authoritarian and more loving than it is. Then we only increase the fear. Those who know that this picture is false will feel threatened by us who hold it as well as by the Soviets.

Let us have faith that candid examination promotes understanding, and that understanding promotes peace.

----

*The term "evil empire" has a long history. The first documented case occurred with reference to Ivan IV ("The Terrible") in a letter by King Sigismund August of Poland to Queen Elizabeth I of England in 1569 (Bobrick 1987:258-9).

Chapter Ten

Liberation Theology

Liberation Theology was much on the minds of Friends I visited on my third journey. "You speak of change from below," they said, "of poor people organizing to negotiate from strength. Is this not what Liberation Theology preaches? Are you not at one with its basic communities?"

In his authoritative work on Liberation Theology, Phil Berryman (1987:38) tells of basic Christian communities, formed by Catholic clergy and laity, that are designed to avoid the paternalism of the past. In community meetings, peasants learn to understand and fight oppression by self-help and village action.

"In Brazil alone it is estimated that there are more than seventy thousand such communities with a total membership of two and a half million people" (p.63). Many thousands more have been formed in other Latin American countries, including Nicaragua.

One of their functions will be *concientización*, which Berryman describes (p.38) as being "roughly equivalent to 'consciousness-raising.'"

Here he tells of a meeting conducted with peasants in a basic community.

> A typical session might begin with a poster or slide projection, showing, for instance, peasants harvesting a crop. To open the discussion, the leader would simply ask, 'What do we see here?' and encourage people to make observations . . . The leader would strive to have people react to the picture rather than to himself or herself; the picture was a "codification" of their life situation, which they were "decoding" through dialogue. The leader's facilitation style was a reversal of the normal domineering or paternalistic patterns of leadership.

Liberation Theology has brought the Church closer to the poor, showing that there are some who care. Both priests and laity have dedicated themselves unstintingly.

Yet I have two hesitations.

First hesitation: religion and politics

I hesitate about the mixture of religion and politics. Both are valuable. But I am no more happy with the "religionization" of politics than I am with the politicization of religion.

To me, religion is a set of spiritual values undergirding our whole being. Politics is secular action undertaken according to conscience and belief. People of the same religion may have different politics, and people of different religions may have the same politics.

Why are the basic communities *Christian* when many third-world peasants, even in Latin America, are not? The supposition that the Latin American Catholic church is an indigenous force permeating the people needs to be re-examined.

Is there not a possible conflict of interest between religion and politics? *Can* the radical Church be totally selfless and dedicated to the poor, in case the interests of either should depart from the other?

For example, four Catholic priests have accepted high-level positions in the Sandinista government, and many lower-level jobs have gone to priests and nuns (Shea 1987). The base communities, I am told, generally favor the government. Yet the peasantry as a whole is bitterly divided.

Suppose that their congregations should decide that what they most want is peace, no matter which side would win. Would priests-in-government have a conflict of interest if the government does not want peace?

The conflict of interest in history

Such a conflict of interest has occurred historically.

Popular wisdom tells us that until recently the Church in Latin America was handmaiden of the status quo. On the great estates it persuaded the peon farmer to be content with his or her burdens, and he or she would be rewarded in heaven. Liberation Theology, it is said, marks both a new departure and a radicalization of priests and laity.

In fact, this split in the Church dates to the Conquest in the sixteenth century.

As the great estates were formed; as Indians were captured in raids and forced to work on Spanish ranches and to dig in Spanish mines or were run into debt bondage on the estates, some priests connived in these oppressions.

But others declared themselves defenders of the Indians. It is their history that might correspond to Liberation Theology today.

Among these was Bartolomé de Las Casas, a Dominican friar who dedicated his life (c.1474-1566) to the Indians. As an early landowner, he gave "his" Indians back to the Governor in 1514 and returned to Spain to plead for the natural rights of Indians.

In 1519 he persuaded Charles I to form "towns of free Indians" where Spanish and Indians worked side by side. Other priests joined his cause, and many such towns were established in the Spanish and Portuguese possessions.

The experiences of these towns will not coincide exactly with the future of the basic communities of Liberation Theology, because conditions are different today.

But one bridge links the two histories: the interests of the priests were different from those of the Indians in the sixteenth century, and they may not be totally the same as those of the poor today.

Fearing the power of the nobility, Kings Charles I and Philip II supported the Church and the Indians as counterweights to them. As a result, the Indians became pawns in the wars between the Church and other landowners, between the king and the nobility, and between Spaniards and Portuguese in defining the boundaries of Brazil.

Sometimes the Indians rebelled against their priest protectors. Farriss (1984:361) tells how the bishop of Yucatan assumed control over Indian cooperatives, selling the lands of Indians without consulting them.

Sometimes Indians wished to leave the protected areas, but because their "protection" had been complete they had no place to go.

The counterparts today

These elements have their counterparts today, though they are not exactly the same because history always repeats itself a bit differently.

Today, revolutionary governments, successors to the kings, often support the liberation church against the "oligarchy," successors to the nobility. Peasants may well become embroiled in wars of revolution *whether they wish to or not,* just as Indians became involved in the wars of the Church and King in the sixteenth century.

Those Friends of my third journey who favored "just war" saw nothing wrong with this. But a pacifist must hesitate.

The people are put at risk. In the wars of yesteryear, "protected" Indian towns were sacked by Brazilian *bandeirantes,* the pioneers who claimed the interior for the Crown. In Central America today, peasants have been killed because of suspected sympathies with one side or another.

Second hesitation: "cultural superiority"

We in the United States value the precept of equality. The poor differ because they are poor, but in our culture they are not deemed *inferior.*

In most of the third world, however, the peasant masses have been told for generations that they are "culturally inferior" to the urban educated, such as lawyers, professors, government officials, and priests. Both sides have come to believe this difference.

The "culturally superior" tend to believe they are superior in everything, not just in their technical specialties. The minister of finance may think that because he is who he is, he knows more about education than the local schoolmaster. The agricultural officer's advice is to be taken because he is a government functionary, when often he knows less about farming than the farmer does.

Both government officials and university professors call on their "cultural superiority" to justify their authority when their knowledge fails. This is one reason for the "paternalistic patterns of leadership" to which Berryman referred.

Although it is possible for a South American peasant to become a priest, very few do. Virtually all priests are from the intellectual, educated classes.

Catholic priests and laity and sincere North American visitors may be listened to as "cultural superiors" and not as persons possessing the skills that peasants need. Organizations they suggest, such as basic communities, may be adopted for the same reason.

I fear that practitioners of Liberation Theology may unknowingly disparage centuries of indigenous communities by forming new ones. I fear they may undercut the dignity of traditional village chiefs by supplanting them as leaders. I also fear they will underrate peasant minds by trying to "raise consciousness."

Third-world peasants have their own kinship and clan relationships, their own village meetings and chiefs, their own *barazas* (East African for *powwow*), and their own financial and support networks. Except where the government has forbidden them, they have their own cooperatives.

It is normal for a knowledgeable person to teach another in his or her field of specialty. But it is paternalistic for a "cultural superior" to "raise the consciousness" of a whole *class* of people.

Let us start with what peasants have. Let the priests offer themselves to existing networks, on peasant terms, instead of creating new "communities" by the thousands after models set by the clergy.

Can peasants organize themselves?

Marxist historian Hobsbawm (1974:120-151) has argued persuasively that Latin American peasants are more capable than any non-peasant to judge what revolutionary action they may take and when it will be successful.

He tells (p.133) how Peruvian Indians, given arms in the War of the Pacific (1879-1884) to fight the Chileans, seized upon the opportunity to fight the landowners instead.

He also tells (p.137) how Indians preserved documents proving land rights granted by the king of Spain in the sixteenth century, to present in law courts of the twentieth century, and *in some cases they won.*

Who says that peasants who can save documents for four centuries to present them in a modern court and win their cases need to have new communities formed and their consciences raised by persons who are not peasants?

Don't the peasants see through it all?

But if the peasants are so "street wise," don't they see through the nonsense of "cultural superiority?" Don't they recognize that "cultural superiors" do not know more than they do on *everything?* Why do they go along with the ways that "superiors" suggest, at the risk of emasculating their own ways?

This has been one of the most difficult imponderables for me. Since I cannot put myself into the mind of a Latin American peasant, I cannot tell.

I suspect they *do* see through it all, and I have two *guesses* about why they conform.

The first is that they see the "success" of the "cultural superiors." There *must* be something they have, the peasant may be thinking, and if I listen long enough, I will find out what it is.

But the second guess seems more probable. During the centuries that opportunities have been denied them, peasants have learned that the way to obtain resources is to do what "superiors" say.

In most of the third world, resources come from "connections," especially with the government. They may come through subsidies or by manipulation of prices, such as bus fares. Soon or later, these "superiors" will intercede for them with the government, bringing them favors that only they, the "superiors," can arrange.

But how can we interact?

So, how can we interact with the poor as equals when we are always taken, at first, to be "cultural superiors?"

We may walk humbly among them if we are able. We may stand by, listen, and learn from them. We may sift their requests, which will come by the hundreds, and decide in which ones we will interact. The Friends World Committee on Consultation (FWCC) is doing just that.

Those of us who cannot go to the poor may support those who do, financially if we are able, spiritually in any event.

We may tell them things we know without suggesting that it is we who have the answers. We may also ask them questions, so that teaching is two-way. We should not "teach" what does not arise out of their questions.

We may visit existing communities instead of forming new ones. We would not portray "their life situation" for them to "decode," as if we knew the code and they did not.

Besides, "their life situation" as depicted by the "cultural superior" may be so different from their own perception of it that our poster or slide show would be off the mark.

None of these reservations contradicts my support for religious leaders coming close to the community or for indigenous political action to take place.

But, to summarize, these are the dangers I see:

First, the mixture of religion and politics, which history has repeatedly shown to corrupt both. The association of part of the Church with revolutionary governments will cause a conflict of interest if the people want peace.

Second, the "cultural superiority" implied in *concientización.*

It would be in the tradition of Friends to wander among the poor, respecting them as equals, asking what is on their minds, learning from them, and searching in silent worship for guidance.

Chapter Eleven

The Third World:

Forgive Them Their Debts?

As 1988 began, the third world owed $1.190 trillion to the industrialized world. Interest and amortization payments were crushing. For some countries, half or more of their export earnings is obligated to creditors, leaving only the rest to pay for needed imports.

To cover interest and payments due on their debts, governments have increased taxes where that was politically feasible. Where it was not, they have printed money, causing unprecedented inflation, such as over 1000% in a year in Argentina and Bolivia.

When governments exchange the newly-printed money for foreign currency to pay the debt, they cause the exchange rate to plummet. The Mexican peso, which was worth 12 to the dollar only a few years ago, dropped to over 2,500 to the dollar in 1987.

Ordinary citizens paid enormous prices for imported goods. In 1987, Brazil, Peru, and Ecuador announced they could not pay their debts as scheduled. Unilaterally they decreased their payments.

The crush was upon the poor. When most business is owned by the government, the main way to scrape up cash is to keep down wages. Government decrees limited private wages too, to lessen inflation.

What little money was left in the pockets of the poor lost its value, as prices of food and shelter skyrocketed, while wages did not. In these ways, the real goods with which the debts were being paid were squeezed out of the poor.

"Let us forgive these debts," Friends cried out in anguish. "The poor have suffered enough." This is indeed what some governments have done, such as Sweden. It is what Willy Brandt of West Germany has advocated.

If I did not join the cry for forgiveness, surely here was final proof of my callousness. So when I said, "The best way to serve the poor is to *refuse* to forgive the debts," some Friends could not comprehend my inhumanness.

How did these debts come about, and why have they grown to mountainous proportions? Some debt is quite normal. Since the beginning of industrialization, countries more economically advanced have lent to poorer ones.

Europe lent to America in the early nineteenth century. The United States has lent to Latin America, Britain to the Commonwealth, and France to French-speaking Africa.

Loans and other investments enabled less developed countries to buy capital goods, and with the product of that capital they paid principal and interest. World debt levels were considered reasonable in 1970. In the 1970s, however, third-world borrowing moved to extraordinary levels.

In 1973, the Organization of Petroleum Exporting Countries (OPEC) began increasing the price of oil. Further increases came, at first gradually, then more abruptly. By 1983, the price of Saudi Arabian oil was over 21 times what it had been in 1970.

Consuming countries were immediately hit, especially Japan which produces no oil of its own. The United States and Europe were also affected, as was much of the third world.

Money flowed from Japan, the third world, Europe, and the United States into the treasuries of Mexico, Indonesia, the Middle East, Nigeria, and Venezuela.

The flow was so great that the recipient countries did not know how to spend it all. "Development" was their great cry. Saudi Arabia built airports, tourist hotels, highways, and some new industry. Its government and oil-company officials built luxury homes and drove Mercedes-Benzes.

The Nigerian Government was advised to plant a band of drought-tolerant trees in the North to ward off encroachment by the Sahara. But it was not interested. Instead, it built a new airport, cut the country up with high-speed highways, and started constructing a new, luxurious inland capital, Abuja.

Non-oil-producing countries in the third world could scarcely afford higher prices. New industry was postponed. Farmers newly accustomed to petrochemical fertilizers found them too expensive. In some countries inflation zoomed, agricultural output suffered, and unemployment went up.

OPEC refused to reduce prices for the non-oil third world, but it did announce a loan and grant program, which was almost entirely devoted to Arab League countries, plus Pakistan, in which OPEC had political interests. Others remained deeply hurt.

Despite all the development programs and profligacy of officials, OPEC still could not spend its money fast enough. It needed a haven for dollars left over. The safest places were in Europe and the United States, where funds were put into banks, Treasury bonds, land, and later into all manner of stocks, bonds, and other investments.

So the net flow of money was out of the non-oil third world, via OPEC, into Europe and the United States. The non-oil third world was in crisis. How to get the funds back?

Obvious answer: bank loans. Money from the World Bank, the regional development banks, the International Monetary Fund, and finally, private banks in Switzerland, California, and New York. Thus began the third-world debt crisis.

At first, the loans were thought of as emergency. Once the non-oil third world economies adapted to the higher oil prices, it was thought that they would cut back expenditures and start to repay.

But they did not adapt. They treated the loans like ordinary income, continuing their previous levels of spending. It was hard to fault them, they were so poor.

Toward the end of the 1970s, curiously enough, some oil-exporting countries - Mexico, Venezuela, Nigeria, Indonesia - started borrowing as well. Why, with all the millions flowing in, would they borrow more?

The answer: they forecast still more oil revenue in the future. Mexico had billions of gallons under ground, and it was supposed the bonanza would go on "forever." But politicians were in office only for a limited time. They and their cronies could divert money to their own purposes only if they could skim off the fat now.

Why would foreign banks countenance such borrowings, when banks normally lend only for well-conceived projects which, because they are profitable, are expected to yield the funds for repayment? Why did they not pay attention to time-honored principles?

Three answers: First, bankers considered themselves "good citizens," recycling the funds back to the non-oil third world, which was so much in need. Second, the banks were overflowing with dollars from oil countries, which they had to invest somewhere. Third, the bankers lulled themselves into the belief that "sovereign governments always pay their debts."

Had they read history more carefully, the bankers would have known that bankruptcy for sovereign governments has been common.

The English king went bankrupt in the 1340s. More relevant is the number of times the Spanish king went bankrupt in the seventeenth century, while vast quantities of silver were flowing in from Potosí in Upper Peru (now Bolivia). In our own century before World War II, Germany and Bolivia repudiated debts.

All went precariously well for the third-world debt until the "oil glut" of 1983, when high prices encouraged conservation of oil and production of substitutes (coal, gas, solar energy) and oils harder to extract, which at lower prices would have been left in the ground. So demand for new oil dropped just as supply was burgeoning.

As the price began to fall, oil-producing countries such as Indonesia, Mexico, Nigeria, Peru, and Venezuela couldn't pay their debts.

Yet *none of these countries had much to show for the billions they had borrowed:* few profitable new plants employing the many jobless workers, few improved schools or universities to train the labor force, little farm equipment or new technology to increase the supply of food, few new products for export, to pay the interest and amortize the debt.

Instead, the funds had either been invested in unprofitable showcase monuments or had been doled out to corrupt civil servants.

The balance of payments of Mexico shows a swelling of unexplained outflows of funds in the early eighties that must have been money sent by politicians and their cronies for safekeeping or for buying land in the United States.

Who would benefit if we forgave this debt?

First, the New York and California banks, which loaned so unwisely. The government of the United States would be expected to reimburse them.

Second, the politicians of the third world who boondoggled or stole the funds. They would be released from responsibility.

If we wish to forgive these culprits, have we forgotten the Quaker principle of not entering into debt greater than one can handle? Have we forgotten the many Friends who were disowned from their Meetings for violating this principle?

Their punishment was harsh, but was the Friends' principle of those days wrong? Or do we think, falsely, that it is the poor whose debts would be forgiven? Whoever heard of banks lending to the poor?

The policy of the U.S. Government is vacillating, to "keep things quiet" in the manner described in Chapter 6. Our government encourages private banks to lend more, so that third-world debtors can cover interest even if they don't repay.

Banks resist "throwing good money after bad," but their reward is that our government and international agencies will advance additional funds to lessen the risks of the private banks.

Our government also uses the debt crisis to cajole third-world governments into policies we recommend, such as to sell their nationalized industries into private hands, to reduce price controls, and to liberalize imports.

These are all good policies, but they do not work when viewed as bribery from the United States.

We have also suggested that they sell government debt at a discount to private buyers - Chile has done some of this - but not enough foolhardy investors are available.

More recently, one bank has written off part of its debt from Mexico in exchange for Mexico buying U.S. government securities whose value will increase over twenty years to cover the rest of the debt. But most banks will not do this.

The present policies, which change frequently, keep the debt alive, with the hope that

it will diminish over time with economic growth,
or with inflation, which lowers the value of
dollars to be repaid.

Partial forgiveness would keep it alive
too. But keeping the debt alive will keep the
poor in bondage.

Friends face an intolerable dilemma in
deciding whether to favor forgiveness.

On the one hand, forgiveness protects the
private banks, who are surely to blame for making the loans, and it exonerates greedy, dishon-
est politicians in the third world.

Worse yet, it sets a precedent. It says
politicians can get away with stealing or wast-
ing funds, and it promotes the idea of doing it
again.

On the other hand, without forgiveness,
the poor will suffer the most.

Facing this dilemma, I have concluded that
the best course would be to refuse further post-
ponement and further lending. The governments of
several countries, most likely Mexico and Brazil, would go bankrupt. So also would some large
banks in the United States. Bankruptcy wipes out
debt, but not by forgiveness.

The poor would be instantly relieved, because the governments would no longer be im-
pelled to suck the interest payments out of
them. Taxes could be lowered. More goods would
stay at home for consumption in the third world.

Inflation would be stopped, unless it was started again by the same politicians for their own greed. Export earnings could be used to pay for needed imports.

Official objections to this policy are several.

First, some say that depositors in the lending banks would lose their funds: you and I, who innocently put our money in these banks. But the U.S. government could pay these depositors instead of paying the banks. There is precedent for this in the Federal Deposit Insurance Corporation, although the law would have to be amended to increase the insurable ceiling, now $100,000. The process would not be inflationary, because the new money given to depositors would merely replace the money extinguished by the losses.

Second, the creditworthiness of the third world might be impaired. Of course. But those who fear the results of this have not studied history. Bankrupt clients sometimes do restore their creditworthiness.

I believe that after sovereign governments go bankrupt, banks might be more willing to lend to *private* businesses in the third world, paying attention to the profitability of loans. They might be inclined to lend more for productivity than for sovereignty.

To summarize: If governments go bankrupt, the poor would be relieved of their burden. Those guilty of improvidence or corruption would be more likely to be punished. With some new legislation, the innocent would be protected and the world economy would not suffer.

Why has no one proposed this solution publicly? Because it is not politic to drive our largest banks into bankruptcy or to discredit the governments of Argentina, Brazil, Mexico, and Nigeria.

But Quakers, if our only interest lies in alleviating the intense suffering of the poor, and if we recall our traditions, might give it some thought.

Appendix

In 1977, I studied the net flows of funds among OPEC, the non-oil third world, and industrial countries, to investigate whether net flows were from the non-oil third world, via OPEC, to Europe and the United States. The results, with data, are published in my article, "The Oil Price Increase: Impacts on Industrialized and Less-Developed Countries," in *The Journal of Energy and Development,* Autumn, 1977. I have not done first-hand research since that time, but I have followed the writings of others.

Current events on foreign debt can be followed in *World Debt Tables,* published periodically by the World Bank; in *IMF Survey,* a bi-weekly publication of the International Monetary Fund; in the *Annual Reports* of the International Monetary Fund and the World Bank; and in articles in the *Washington Post, New York Times,* and *Wall Street Journal.*

Chapter Twelve

Profits

In Chapter 16 of *Facing Social Revolution,* I wrote of profit in its "real" (as opposed to "financial") form: the goods and services that "real" capital - machines, buildings, ports, highways, and the like - makes.

If labor makes more with a machine (capital) than without, the additional product is profit of capital. An economy with machines and buildings earns profit, whether it is socialist, cooperative, capitalist, or whatever.

We cannot abolish profit, and it does no good to call it "evil."

But I also explained how, in Western society, the capitalist (owner of the machine) over time has paid out much of the increased profit to the worker in wages, as he *must* where labor is in high demand.

In this way, with a few temporary exceptions, for the past 150 years real wages (the goods that money wages can buy) per hour of labor have increased while real interest and dividends, as percentage of capital invested, have remained almost constant.

Total profits have risen, but not at the expense of wages. Rather, wages and profits rise together.

Some Friends of my third journey were not satisfied with this explanation because I had not paid attention to greed.

"Christmas should be a time of joy," one Friend said, "but I am saddened as I watch profit-seekers distort its spirit with gaudy displays and raucous music."

"In search of profit," another went on, "companies sell toys that teach war to children. Sometimes the toys explode and kill the children."

Another went on: "We sell munitions to the third world to make profit." Still another spoke of American companies selling business machines to the South African government, profiting as the police state becomes more efficient.

Friends found no quarrel from me on these charges, for I agreed with them all.

However, I sometimes felt Friends perceived profit as the offspring of greed, and they were trying to fob off greed as a monster apart from ourselves.

The monster, rather than people, was to blame for defiling Christmas, for making toys that kill, and for selling business machines to the police state. "Were it not for this monster," Friends *seemed* to be saying, "people would not do these things."

Then I thought of my shoemaker. His business is not gaudy. Day in and day out he sits in his shop, mending shoes. He could have put his money in the bank to earn interest.

But he invested it in shoe-repair machines instead. Should he not earn a profit to compensate for the interest he is missing? He doesn't sell to a police state. He keeps my feet warm.

I thought of hundreds of other people. The huckster and the ice man who came to my house when I was a child. Their capital was horse and wagon. One brought vegetables and the other what we needed to keep them fresh.

Then my mind jumped half a century to the company that makes my word processor, with which I write this book. Also the light-bulb company, the furniture company, the egg farmer, and so on down a long list. They all use machinery that earns profit. Do they all do what they do because they are greedy?

Profit is the return on real capital, or machines. It is also the *feedback* on what people want.

What kinds of machines we make and what we do with them are up to us. Many businesspeople, probably most, earn profit in wholesome ways.

But profit is not the first inanimate idea on which I have heard people blame our personal faults. Others include multinational corporations and capitalism.

Let us think of these entities as generic or neutral, and let us ourselves accept responsibility for how we use them.

Let us examine our Inner Lights to determine whether and how we defile Christmas, harm South Africans, or make war.

Or instead, do we make shoes, deliver vegetables and eggs, light bulbs, furniture, and those things that make life wholesome? Not whether we seek profit, but which way do we seek it?

Most Friends are acquainted with Adam Smith, who wrote of the invisible hand, in *The Wealth of Nations* (1776):

> Every individual endeavors to employ his capital so that the produce of the day may be of greatest value. He generally neither intends to promote the public interest, nor knows how much he is promoting it. He intends only his own security, only his own gain. And he is led in this by an invisible hand to promote an end which was no part of his intention. By pursuing his own interest he frequently promotes that of society more effectually than when he really intends to promote it.

Smith is telling us that the shoemaker makes shoes, the farmer grows wheat, the computer company makes word processors (pardon the anachronism), and the munitions plant makes guns in response to profit.

Profit in turn responds to what we want. If we do not want munitions, there will be no profit in them. The same is so for shoes, eggs, wheat, and all the rest.

Two centuries later, Paul Samuelson used the same example, in his famous textbook, *Economics*, to explain why every store in New York City receives, daily, just the amount of milk it needs. The shelves rarely lack milk, yet little spoils from daily overages.

In an unplanned economy, the profit "feedback" directs how much we will produce and where it will go. Competition keeps price and profit from being excessive.

Not only can our economy not function without profit as a bellweather, but neither can the Soviet nor the Chinese nor the Nicaraguan economy. The failures of socialism result in part from lack of feedback on which goods are wanted and which methods are efficient.

I also believe that individuals are motivated not solely by profit, but by values.

I do not teach because I make more money that way. I passed my CPA exams in 1950 and turned my back on a profession in which I could have earned much more than I do now.

I did not write *Facing Social Revolution* for profit. Therefore I was not disappointed when none came.

So what about the shoemaker, the egg farmer, or even the munitions maker? Am I so arrogant as to believe that only teachers value what we are doing?

Let us, for the moment, examine a world without profit, the third world that we visited in Chapter 11 on debt. There, borrowing politicians could waste the proceeds precisely because they did not have to yield a tangible return on investment. They borrowed from international banks and invested the funds in personal consumption or in grandiose enterprises that failed.

They were not held accountable. Their governments did not judge them, nor were there any stockholders, nor a board of trustees, to say, "Don't use the money that way, because it does not yield a profit."

In the spirit of Clarence Pickett, who is credited with saying, "Sit lightly upon your possessions," let us think of our resources as we think of ourselves.

Let us put ourselves and our capital into actions we believe in. Let us also value the work and the investment that earn us money.

If our values include making peace and feeding the poor, let us do that. But some of us must use ourselves and our machines to keep the wheels turning, to grow wheat, to make shoes and computers, and to put out fires. There is work and profit in all of them.

If others spend their work and their machines making munitions or gaudy Christmases, it is their values and the values of those who demand these products that are to blame, not "profit" or "capitalism."

Let us help them change their values. Let us help them seek profit in more wholesome ways.

Appendix

To show that corporate profits were not as high as is often believed, in *Facing Social Revolution* I compared earnings with net equity as shown on corporate balance sheets. For example, if the original investment in a company is $1,000 and the profit is $100, its rate of profit is 10%. In fact, however, during inflation the real rate of profit is less, because the investment ($1,000) is valued at the lower prices of an earlier year while the return is valued at higher, current prices. If because of inflation the current $100 yield is worth only $50 in earlier-year prices, then the real profit rate is only 5%, or 50/1,000. This is the rate the company would take into account if it were to expand, because today it would have to invest $2,000 in order to earn $100 a year, or 5%. General rule: the real percentage must be calculated with both numerator and denominator in same-year prices.

Something like this has, in fact, happened in the United States, and real corporate profits are lower than what I showed in *Facing Social Revolution.* Comparing net equity at earlier-year prices with net profit at current-year prices (the "wrong way") for all manufacturing corporations in the United States, we find rates of 13.9% in 1980, 10.5% in 1983, 12.5% in 1984, and 10.1% in 1985 (USDC 1987:522). However, according to Department of Commerce figures not available when I wrote *Facing Social Revolution,* the real profit on all corporate assets in the United States has declined from about 8% in the mid-1960s to about 3 1/2% in the late 1970s and early 1980s (Uchitelle 1987:1). It started to rebound in 1983 but had reached only 4.2% in 1986. Many corporations would earn greater profits if they sold all their assets and put the money into Treasury notes.

In a textbook on economics, Princeton professors Baumol and Blinder (1979:548) commented on the perceptions of profits by college students, as recorded in a Gallup poll. "Contrary to what the college students who were polled thought, the typical profit margin on sales is closer to 10 percent than to 45 percent, and the typical corporate tax on net earnings of $100,000 is about $42,000, not $15,000." My note: since Baumol and Blinder's book was published, the profit margin on sales has gradually fallen, to 3.8% in 1985 (USDC 1987:522).

How close to the mark are Friends' perceptions of the amount and rate of corporate profit?

Chapter Thirteen

Worker Capitalists

Some Friends of my third journey were still not satisfied with my explanation of profits. Even if profits are essential to supply the right amount of milk to every store in New York, they said, should not the workers own their plants and receive the profits?

Why should an outsider profit just by owning a company, and not working in it?

The idea of worker ownership has been attractive for a long time. John Stuart Mill, economic philosopher of the mid-nineteenth century, advocated it. French socialist Louis Blanc in the 1840s proposed "social workshops" controlled by workers, which would gradually take over all production until socialism was achieved.

Toward the end of that century, German philosopher Otto von Gierke favored worker cooperatives, so that business would serve the person and not vice-versa. Worker ownership is nostalgic of days before the industrial revolution, when craftspeople owned their tools.

Today, the tradition survives. The Moosewood Restaurant in Ithaca, N.Y., is worker-owned and worker-operated. The introduction to *New Recipes from Moosewood Restaurant* tells a story reminiscent of a Quaker business meeting:

> Management decisions are made by group consensus, which at times may seem laborious, but is actually surprisingly effective . . . There's no one boss, much to the wonderment of those who come in asking to see the manager and are shown in to the offices of the dishwasher. We're interested in helping each other, so if your waiter's very busy, the cook may serve your dinner.

The early English factories, many of them Quaker, were family-owned. In an age of huge plants, would not worker ownership be the modern counterpart?

I do not think so. I would distinguish between a small company based on capital scraped up by the present generation and larger companies constructed from inherited capital.

Our high standard of living comes from our high technology, which results from the saving, investment, and inventiveness of our forebears. It is embodied in real capital.

We do not deserve it. It is ours by chance of birth. I would think it only moral that we should use it first as a fund for the poor: social security, unemployment and illness insurance. After that, it should be spread around as widely as possible. That is what I recommended in *Facing Social Revolution.*

Only about one in five of our workers is in manufacturing, where much of the capital lies. Worker ownership would imply that instead of being widely spread or used for the poor, this capital and its profit would belong to this small group.

By contrast, the one out of three workers who are in service industries would own less capital and receive less profit. The unemployed poor, the very ones who should benefit most, would be excluded, because they have no jobs at all.

There are other complications. "If the workers owned all the stock in a plant," I asked Friends during my third journey, "what would happen if a worker quit? Would he take his ownership with him?"

"No," most Friends answered, "for the worker would become an outsider, and outsiders shouldn't own the plant."

"But suppose," I went on, "a worker wants to leave IBM to work for XYZ, because the job at XYZ pays more or provides greater creative scope. But XYZ is earning less profit than IBM. Wouldn't the worker be reluctant to lose his share of the IBM profit?"

"Possibly so," came the answer, "he would have to make his choice." But it seemed to me cruel to penalize a worker for moving where he can be more creative or earn more. Conversely, a worker moving from XYZ to IBM would gain an undeserved bonus.

Another thought. Owning a company is like owning a house or land. It is an investment, and for every investment, someone has saved. The worker/owner might even have his or her life savings invested in the company.

Is it a good idea to invest one's savings in the same company where one works: all eggs in one basket? Suppose the company fails, as did worker-owned People Express. Wouldn't one lose one's job and one's life savings in one blow?

Next, suppose the workers of IBM were offered, free of charge, all the stock of IBM. They would own the company in which they worked. Surely they would be overjoyed.

But suppose instead that they were offered the money value of all IBM stock, and they might buy the stock or not if they liked. Would they do it?

I suspect many would not, for they would prefer a different investment. Worker ownership means that the workers are *required* to invest their funds where they have their jobs, when for security or other reasons they might prefer to put them elsewhere.

For good or for ill, the day of close association of the worker with his tools is past,
except in small businesses like Moosewood. I do
not believe that modern workers feel the same
kinship with blast furnaces and huge building
complexes that the blacksmith did with his
forge.

Instead, it seems to me, the nostalgia for
worker ownership is carried mostly by intellectuals, who deem it wholesome for blue-collar
workers whom they have not consulted.

Let us ponder the case of Yugoslavia,
whose workers not only manage their plants but
even the departments within them. Legally, they
do not own companies, for all are owned by the
state. But they hire and fire the managers, determine their own wages, and decide what to do
with profits.

What have been the results? Bordewich
(1986) reports:

>Inefficiency and apathy have
>reached astonishing proportions.
>According to Western estimates, more
>than a quarter of the 6 million
>workers in the public sector are
>unnecessary. On any given day,
>700,000 workers are "on sick leave"
>and 600,000 more "on vacation."
>Those who show up work an average of
>3.5 hours a day; despite new machin-
>ery, it takes, for example, 1,500
>man-hours to build a railway car
>that in 1970 took 1,000.

Newman (1987) reports the following about strikes in Yugoslavia:

> In the city of Maribor, the doctors went out last year; so did the vegetable vendors. In Split, on the Adriatic, 6,000 workers shut the shipyard and 140 bus drivers stranded 150,000 riders. Coal miners and millhands and schoolteachers struck. So did the clerical staff of Croatia's Parliament. Close to 800 wildcat strikes hit Yugoslavia in 1986, twice 1984's number. Around 80,000 workers took part.
>
> This month, things have suddenly become even worse. A wave of strikes has clobbered the country in response to the government's feeble efforts to impose some restraints on wages. In Croatia, walkouts reportedly forced 40 factories to close.

But if workers manage the business, against whom are they striking?

Against the state. Since the beginning of self-management under Tito, workers have reinvested little in their plants. They have voted themselves higher wages than plant income could afford, borrowing the difference.

The result: inflation. Prices are now rising by 140% per year (Diehl 1987:21), the highest rate in Europe.

To keep the inflation from increasing further, the government borrowed from abroad. Yugoslavia now owes more than $20 billion to foreign governments and banks, which puts it among the world's heaviest debtors in proportion to population and income.

To end this bankrupting cycle, the government has tried to limit wage increases. Against that, the workers are striking.

Not all the disaster is attributable to worker management. Ethnic violence, such as between Albanians and Slavs in Kosovo; the inability of federated republics to cooperate and the absence of central coordination; trade barriers of republics to keep out the goods of other republics; and government regulations of the types I have described for the third world - all play a part.

But the main reason, it seems to me, is that management is a specialized skill. It should be entrusted to trained, salaried persons who are responsible, not to workers, but to those whose sole stake is in the success of the enterprise, undiluted by an interest in wages.

Individually, many Yugoslav workers are aware of this, and some are voting to relinquish their powers. "Even the workers want discipline," Radmilla Nakarada, Belgrade sociologist, told a Western reporter. "They're hungry for management."

Some 7,000 plants in the United States are now owned, all or in part, by their employees. Worker ownership is obviously possible, but I have not yet seen a good study on how successful it is or how it meets worker aspirations.

Sometimes workers buy a failing company to preserve their jobs, as did those of Hyatt Clark Industries, producers of ball bearings, in 1981.

Off to a poor start, beleaguered by continued management problems, they lost both their jobs and their savings when the company went under in 1987.

When people who have already adopted values of cooperation, of love, and of sitting lightly on our possessions voluntarily form a workers' cooperative, then we get a Moosewood.

But when workers buy their plants in desperation, or when cooperatives are imposed upon them by politicians who believe "cooperatives are good for workers," then we get a Yugoslavia.

How were social institutions forged in our own country, or in Britain, France, the Soviet Union, China, Nicaragua, Tanzania, or others? When Friends say we "favor" workers' cooperatives, which way of forming them do we mean?

As Friends dream of a "new society," let us focus first on the values of those who will shape it, second on the next incremental change, and only last on what the new structure will look like.

People forge social institutions as the way opens, according to their values. Institutions theoretically devised and installed by force are destroyed by force, for they have made a value of force, not of love.

We are a long way from universal worker capitalism.

Chapter Fourteen

Food First

"Feed the hungry first. Export later." This cry came from many Friends of my third journey. "Why do the poor of the third world grow coffee, cotton, sugar, and tomatoes for export to the United States, when they themselves are starving? What do you think of Food First?

I have great sympathy for Food First, and I recommend that every Friend read *World Hunger: Ten Myths*, by the authors of *Food First*, Frances Moore Lappé and Joseph Collins. Here, Lappé and Collins cite ten widely-held beliefs about food, every one of which is false. Among these is myth no. 7 (p.27):

> If countries where so many go hungry did not produce agricultural exports, then the land now growing for foreign consumers would nourish local people. Export agriculture, therefore, is the enemy.

"Export agriculture is *not* the enemy," Lappé and Collins assert. But they point out that in many third-world countries the state is

biased toward exports because it can more easily
extort export earnings than it can those from
foodstuffs for home consumption.

It wants the foreign exchange, which it
gets by capturing the agricultural surplus
through price controls and forced procurement.

But why is not export agriculture *also* the
enemy? Why shouldn't the people grow food for
themselves rather than for us? For the same reason that you and I don't grow our own food
(usually) but take other jobs instead.

The problem is not one of getting food to
the people but of getting *income* to the poor,
with which they can buy food.

Often small farmers might obtain *more* corn
and beans for their families if, instead of
growing them, they grow coffee for export, sell
it on the international market, and buy corn and
beans with the proceeds. The catch is that the
state often deprives them of much of the
proceeds.

So *state control* of farming is the enemy,
not export agriculture. The answer is to take
the restraints off farmers and let them decide
whether to grow for export or home consumption
according to profitability. Note *profitability*
as an economic indicator, not as a token of
greed.

My only disagreement with Lappé and
Collins is their apparent belief, which comes
out in their other writings, that socialist gov-

ernments do not *also* deprive the farmer of the surplus.

Indeed, the governments of socialist China, Cuba, Ethiopia, Nicaragua, Tanzania, and the Soviet Union all impose forced procurement at prices unfavorable to the farmer, just as do the governments of non-socialist Egypt, India, Kenya, Mexico, Pakistan, and Paraguay.

Those who favor the rural poor will, if possible, *help the farmer get land of his or her own;* help him or her gain access to *normal* channels of credit, not subsidized state credit, which always has a "hitch" to it; make agricultural extension available but *not force it;* and allow the farmer to obtain seed, fertilizer, and other inputs *on the free market* instead of requiring purchases from the state.

These are to me the requisites of "food first."

One frustrated Turkish farmer put the matter concisely to a University of Wisconsin land-reform researcher (Lemel 1977:10):

"Just give us the land and leave us alone."

Chapter Fifteen

Pacifism, Peace, and Justice

"If you want peace, seek justice." So read the bumper sticker at a Friends' gathering.

I have heard the expression "peace and justice" so often that I have begun to wonder if it was one word, "peacenjustice." What is peace? What is justice?

I thought about how I was a conscientious objector in World War II. Did we refuse to fight Germany because it was a country of justice? A country that had overrun Europe, gassed Jews wholesale, tortured and murdered?

At that time, it was *nonpacifists* who were saying, "If you want peace, seek justice," or, "justice comes first, then peace." The corollary was, "this war is a just war." Was *that* the message of the bumper sticker?

My thoughts went back further, to 1936. I was in high school, and all my friends were for peace. No one wanted another world war. Then I remembered 1940. I was in college, the war in Europe had begun, and my friends increasingly thought the United States should re-arm.

I debated a classmate who said, "Better have the draft and not need it than need it and not have it." I said, "Having it will make us need it."

But popularity swung his way. My Class of 1941 was the last to graduate in America's peacetime, and most of my classmates went off to war.

When still I refused, among shrinking ranks, I sought a people who might find unity with a pacifist in a world of injustice.

Members of the Society of Friends were the only ones who did so while also practicing a religion that I found appealing.

When asked how I could be pacifist while my compatriots were "doing my fighting for me," my answer came in two parts.

The first drew on Thoreau, Gandhi, and other advocates of nonviolent resistance. Nonviolent resisters, I said, would throw themselves in front of oncoming tanks and would refuse to cooperate in any way with invaders.

"German soldiers could not survive in France," I went on, "if the French at every point stood in their way, would not feed them, run trains for them, wind up the gas pumps, act as their secretaries, and keep the electricity plants running."

"The Germans would kill the French if they refused to do those things," my challengers would say.

"Did I say we wouldn't get killed in nonviolent resistance?" I would answer. "People get killed in war, too."

Still, nonviolent resistance was theoretical. How could one practice it in the midst of war? How could one confront injustice with pacifism when success depended on everyone doing it, and others would not?

The second part addressed that question. "If there is a way in nonviolence, I must not be deterred from it because others, employing violence, have closed that way momentarily."

Then, by way of afterthought: "Especially in time of war, some must keep alive the word of peace." Later I decided the afterthought was the main message.

Pacifism has two parts, one from the Latin, *pax,* or peace, and the other from *facere,* to make. A pacifist is one who makes peace.

Making peace is more than not making war. It springs from faith that there is always a peaceful way to resolve injustice, and further, that only by the peaceful way will the resolution last. It takes on an active dimension, expressed in love, compromise, and *po'le po'le,* as the Swahili would say, "slowly slowly."

Pacifism never says, "We tried peaceful protest for ten years, or twenty years, and it didn't work." Instead, Pacifism sees back thousands of years, to the uselessness, the perverseness, and the gross destruction of war.

Pacifism feels anguish for the sufferings of the centuries, both those that have passed and those yet to come.

Pacifism sees the many years of peace that have punctuated our world of war, and how justice springs from true peace, not the other way around.

Pacifism does not wonder, "When these people - Central Americans, Vietnamese, or whoever - have suffered so much from my country, how can I tell them not to fight?" for Pacifism acts by precept, not by telling.

Pacifism does not say "seek justice, and you will have peace," for it knows that justice is precarious, always being attacked by people of violence. The mere achievement of justice is never a promise of peace.

Pacifism understands how the peoples of Cambodia, Central America, Ethiopia, Mozambique, and Lebanon suffer more from war than they ever did from injustice. It does not accept rebels for their political aims, often called "justice," but for what they do.

While the Ethiopian Government uses starvation as a weapon against Eritreans and Eritreans do the same against the government;

while the Contras destroy farms to prevent them from feeding the people of Nicaragua; while Salvadoran rebels blow up bridges and electricity plants to paralyze a nation already tired and hungry, Pacifism recognizes that depriving people of their livelihoods is only a short step from depriving them of their lives.

Economic sanctions differ quantitatively from acts of physical violence, but they are the opposite of Pacifism, which nonviolently resists aggression against oneself but does not commit it against others.

Pacifism understands how the seemingly intractable injustices in all the places mentioned can be resolved in peaceful ways and only in peaceful ways, for only by peace have similar injustices been resolved in the historic past.

It sees how war re-creates injustice, only in a new guise.

So which should we seek first, peace or justice?

But rather seek ye the kingdom
of God, and all these things shall
be added unto you (Luke 12:31).

References Cited

Atkinson, Dorothy, 1983:
   The End of the Russian Land Commune, 1905-1930,
   Stanford, CA, Stanford University Press.

Andersen, Alfred F., 1985:
   Liberating the Early American Dream, Ukiah, CA, Tom
   Paine Institute.

Baumol, William J., and Blinder, Alan S., 1979:
   Economics: Principles and Policy, New York, Harcourt
   Brace Jovanovich.

Berryman, Phillip, 1987:
   Liberation Theology, New York, Pantheon Books.

Bobrick, Benson, 1987:
   *Fearful Majesty: The Life and Reign of Ivan the
   Terrible,* New York, G.P. Putnam's Sons.

Bordewich, Fergus M., 1986:
   "Yugoslavia Since Tito," *New York Times Magazine,*
   April 13, p.54ff.

Buck, John Lossing, 1937:
   Land Utilization in China, Nanking, University of
   Nanking, republished by Paragon Book Reprint, New
   York, 1968.

Butterfield, Fox, 1987:
   "Mao and Deng: Competition for History's Judgment,"
   New York Times, November 15.

Conquest, Robert, 1986:
  The Harvest of Sorrow: Soviet Collectivization and the Terror Famine, New York, Oxford University Press.

Davidson, Joe, 1988:
  "Tanzania is Reviving its Economy by Using Tools of a Free Market," *Wall Street Journal*, January 27.

Diehl, Jackson, 1987:
  "Once Again, Yugoslavia is Leading the Way," *Washington Post Weekly*, December 14, p.21.

Farriss, Nancy M., 1984:
  Maya Society under Colonial Rule: The Collective Enterprise of Survival, Princeton, N.J., Princeton University Press.

FAO = Food and Agriculture Organization (United Nations), 1987:
  Yearbook of Agricultural Production, Rome.

Hobsbawm, E.J., 1974:
  "Peasant Land Occupations," *Past and Present*, no. 62, February, pp. 120-152.

International Labor Organization, 1976:
  Wages and Working Conditions in Multinational Corporations, Geneva.

Johnson, D. Gale, and Brooks, Karen McConnell, 1983:
  Prospects for Soviet Agriculture in the 1980s, Bloomington, IN, Indiana University Press, for The Center for Strategic and International Studies, Georgetown University.

Lappé, Frances Moore, and Collins, Joseph, 1982:
    World Hunger: 10 Myths, San Francisco CA, Institute
    for Food and Development Policy.

Lardy, Nicholas R., 1983:
    Agriculture in China's Modern Economic Development,
    Cambridge, Cambridge University Press.

Lemel, Harold, 1977:
    "Examination of the 1973 Turkish Land and Agrarian
    Reform and its Implication: Observations in the Pi-
    lot Province of Urfa, 1977," Madison, WI, University
    of Wisconsin, *Land Tenure Center Newsletter*, no. 58.

Loehr, William, and Powelson, John P., 1983:
    Threat to Development: Pitfalls of the NIEO, Boulder
    CO, Westview Press.

MacFahrquhar, Roderick, 1974:
    *The Origins of the Cultural Revolution: 1:
    Contradictions Among the People, 1956-1657*, New
    York, Columbia University Press.

Moosewood Collective, 1987:
    New Recipes from Moosewood Restaurant, Berkeley CA,
    Ten Speed Press.

Newman, Barry, 1987:
    "Yugoslavia's Workers Find Self-Management Doesn't
    Make Paradise," *Wall Street Journal*, March 25.

Pear, Robert, 1987:
    "Poverty Rate Dips as the Median Family Income
    Rises," *New York Times*, July 31.

Perkins, Dwight H., 1969:
    Agricultural Development in China, 1368-1968,
    Chicago, Aldine Publishing Company, for Social
    Science Research Council.

Powelson, Jack, 1983:
    Holistic Economics and Social Protest, Wallingford,
    PA, Pendle Hill Pamphlet no. 252.

Powelson, John P., and Stock, Richard, 1987:
    *The Peasant Betrayed: Agriculture and Land Reform in
    the Third World,* Lincoln Institute of Land Policy,
    26 Trowbridge Street, Cambridge, MA 02138.

Powelson, John P., 1988:
    *The Story of Land: A World History of Land Tenure
    and Agrarian Reform,* Lincoln Institute of Land
    Policy, 26 Trowbridge Street, Cambridge, MA 02138.

Rosenberg, Nathan, and Birdzell, L.E., Jr., 1986:
    *How the West Grew Rich: The Economic Transformation
    of the Industrial World,* New York, Basic Books.

Shea, Nina Hope, 1987:
    "The Systematic Destruction of Faith in Nicaragua,"
    Wall Street Journal, May 22.

Tawney, R.H., 1932:
    Land and Labour in China, London, George Allen and
    Unwin.

Tregarthen, Timothy, 1987:
    "China's Uneasy March toward Reform," *The Margin,*
    vol. 3, no. 4, December.

Uchitelle, Louis, 1987:
   "Corporate Profitability Rising, Reversing 15-Year
   Downturn," *New York Times,* November 30.

USDC (U.S. Department of Commerce), 1987:
   Statistical   Abstract   of   the   United   States,
   Washington, D.C., Government Printing Office.

Index